VALHALLA

BY PAUL RUDNICK

DRAMATISTS
PLAY SERVICE
INC.

SPECIAL NOTE

Anyone receiving permission to produce VALHALLA is required to give credit to the Author as sole and exclusive Author of the Play on the title page of all programs distributed in connection with performances of the Play and in all instances in which the title of the Play appears for purposes of advertising, publicizing or otherwise exploiting the Play and/or a production thereof. The name of the Author must appear on a separate line, in which no other name appears, immediately beneath the title and in size of type equal to 50% of the size of the largest, most prominent letter used for the title of the Play. No person, firm or entity may receive credit larger or more prominent than that accorded the Author. The following acknowledgment must appear on the title page in all programs distributed in connection with performances of the Play:

VALHALLA was originally presented
by New York Theatre Workshop,
James C. Nicola, Artistic Director,
Lynn Moffatt, Managing Director.

In addition, if the CD below is used in performances, the following acknowledgment must appear on the title page in all programs in size of type equal to that used for the production designers:

Sound design and original music by Mark Bennett.

SPECIAL NOTE ON MUSIC

A CD of the sound design and original music composed for this play by Mark Bennett is available through the Play Service for $35.00, which includes shipping. The nonprofessional fee for the use of this music is $20.00 per performance.

For Christopher Ashley

INTRODUCTION

Valhalla emerged from my lifelong fascination with Ludwig of Bavaria, a gloriously romantic figure known, tellingly, as both the Dream King and the Mad King. Ludwig was born in 1845, and ascended to the throne at nineteen; he died in 1886. From birth, Ludwig's storybook imagination was wildly unfettered; as an adult, he befriended composer Richard Wagner, many of whose greatest operas were written under Ludwig's patronage. Wagner has commented that Ludwig was not particularly musical: The young King loved not so much the arias as the stories of Lohengrin and the Ring, with their brave, doomed heroes and yearning, innocent maidens. Ludwig longed to live within these legendary, fairy-tale worlds, and to an extraordinary degree, he did.

Ludwig was not, technically, a successful monarch, as he completely lacked any administrative or diplomatic skills. He eventually withdrew from his more public duties, and pursued his true dream: building castles. Ludwig hired stage designers to create gorgeous palaces, hunting lodges and theaters based on Wagner's operas, and his passion consumed him. Eventually he ran out of money, and the Bavarian Parliament had Ludwig declared insane and taken off the throne. The next day his body was found in the lake beside one of his beloved castles. The exact nature of Ludwig's death remains a mystery. Many historians regard it as a suicide, while others argue that Ludwig may have been swimming across the water as a means of escape and drowned. Ludwig's madness is also an open question. While his behavior was extreme, it may not have been pathological. To me, Ludwig is a hero, perhaps because in pursuit of his stunningly theatrical dreams, he risked madness.

Most of the information about Ludwig contained in *Valhalla* is true; there are also many worthwhile biographies available, including Greg King's *The Mad King* and Wilfred Blunt's *The Dream King*. But ultimately, I wrote *Valhalla* to be enjoyed by both Ludwig fans and those who've never heard of him and might have no interest in opera or Bavarian politics. I wanted to write about why I find Ludwig such an intriguing and inspiring figure and about why he matters to me and, God willing, the audience. And that's why I created James Avery, a Texas teenager from the 1940s, whose life story runs parallel to Ludwig's until their passionate natures eventually intersect. I wanted to show how two characters who could never really meet might still become soulmates.

Valhalla is about madness and beauty and going too far, and while the play includes tragic elements, it's not about regret. Ludwig and James both want everything, and their dreams are both majestic and dangerous. I wrote the play over a period of several years, and its earliest productions were superbly directed by Christopher Ashley. Here are a few of the things I learned during this process:

• The play must move rapidly and fluidly, using as little cumbersome scenery as possible. The costumes should indicate the various time periods, and the characters' ages. The play's premiere at the New York Theatre Workshop featured a beautiful, deceptively simple set by Thomas Lynch; it appeared to be a bare stage with two columns, one of industrial brick and the other ornate and gilded. William Ivey Long's dazzling costumes took us from Dainsville to Versailles. The extremely quick changes were especially helpful, as when the actress playing Sally, the prettiest girl in Texas, exited and returned seconds later as Princess Sophie, the loneliest humpback in Europe. Kenneth Posner's lighting was absolutely miraculous, particularly in the play's concluding castles sequence.

• The play requires a sustained musical score. Mark Bennett's sound design for the original production was enthralling. Mark's work and his melody for "Soldiers and Seamen" are available from DPS.

• The play's dialogue and action must be immaculately choreographed, particularly in the sections where the two worlds intertwine. Both the wedding at the end of the first act and the castles sequence in Act Two are extremely challenging; the crosscutting should ultimately appear effortless.

• While many of the characters and plot developments in *Valhalla* are extreme, the acting style should remain committed and emotional; everything should be played for keeps and not mere burlesque. The assignment of actors playing multiple roles is also not arbitrary; it's important that we see the same performers playing complementary roles in both Bavaria and Texas.

• A note on accents: The Dainsville characters can use appropriately Texan accents. The Bavarian characters should use Mid-Atlantic accents, except where otherwise indicated in the script.

Within weeks after Ludwig's death, his castles were opened to the public as tourist attractions, and they remain overwhelmingly popular. One of Ludwig's creations, Neuschwanstein, served as the basis for Cinderella's castle at Disneyland. There's clearly something about Ludwig's dreams that bewitches just about everyone. Maybe *Valhalla* is a mad play about a mad king, or maybe it's about the price of orgasmic beauty. But here's what I know for sure: I love Ludwig.

—Paul Rudnick

VALHALLA was originally produced at New York Theatre Workshop (James C. Nicola, Artistic Director; Lynn Moffat, Managing Director) in New York City, opening on February 5, 2004. It was directed by Christopher Ashley; the set design was by Thomas Lynch; the lighting design was by Kenneth Posner; the sound design was by Mark Bennett; the costume design was by William Ivey Long; the choreography was by Daniel Pelzig; and the production stage manager was Sarah Bittenbender. The cast was as follows:

HENRY LEE STAFFORD /
HELMUT / OPERA SINGER .... Scott Barrow

MARGARET AVERY / QUEEN MARIE /
PRINCESS ENID / NATALIE KIPPELBAUM ...... Candy Buckley

JAMES AVERY .... Sean Dugan

KING LUDWIG OF BAVARIA .... Peter Frechette

SALLY MORTIMER / PRINCESS SOPHIE /
PRINCESS PATRICIA / MARIE ANTOINETTE /
ANNIE AVERY .... Samantha Soule

FOOTMAN / OTTO / PFEIFFER /
PRINCESS URSULA THE UNUSUAL /
REVEREND HOWESBERRY /
SERGEANT .... Jack Willis

CHARACTERS

The play is performed by six actors, with four of the actors playing multiple roles as indicated.

LUDWIG

JAMES AVERY

HENRY LEE STAFFORD / HELMUT /
OPERA SINGER

MARGARET AVERY / QUEEN MARIE /
PRINCESS ENID / NATALIE KIPPELBAUM

SALLY MORTIMER / PRINCESS PATRICIA /
PRINCESS SOPHIE / MARIE ANTOINETTE /
ANNIE AVERY

PFEIFFER / OTTO / FOOTMAN /
PRINCESS URSULA THE UNUSUAL /
REVEREND HOWESBERRY / SERGEANT

VALHALLA

ACT ONE

Ludwig of Bavaria runs onstage, dressed in a blue velvet Little Lord Fauntleroy suit and a long curled wig. He will be played by an adult actor, but he's currently ten years old. Ludwig is passionate, highly strung and does not censor his more hallucinatory urges; he's also a true and enduring innocent. The year is 1855.

LUDWIG. I am out of my mind! With excitement! I'm only ten years old, and I've fallen in love! And today — I'm going to tell her! *(James Avery appears. He stares yearningly at a small, beautiful crystal swan located nearby. James will be played by an adult actor, but he's currently ten years old, and he's dressed like a ragged small-town boy from 1930s Texas. James' personality is already fully formed. He's a self-styled aristocrat, and he can be seductive, charming and ruthless. James intends to live a life of enormous possibility, and nothing can stop him.)*

JAMES. *(Staring at the crystal swan.)* It's happenin' again. I'm only ten years old and I shouldn't even be in this department store, 'cause I'm gettin' all itchy. Because I need it!

LUDWIG. I ran all the way down here, to the lake by my family's castle. *(Looking out, towards the audience.)* And here she comes, she's moving like a sunbeam on glass …

JAMES. She's one-hundred-percent fine lead crystal, all the way from Europe …

LUDWIG. She's so perfect …

JAMES. She's so beautiful …

LUDWIG. She's so snooty …

LUDWIG and JAMES. She's a swan!

LUDWIG. And we'll get married, in a grand royal wedding, Prince Ludwig and his bride …

JAMES. And I'll keep you safe in my pocket, and then I'll put you high on my shelf ...

LUDWIG. And we'll talk about everything, about why everyone thinks I'm so incredibly weird, and about why they're all wrong, maybe ...

JAMES. And you will fill my whole room, the whole house, you will fill my whole life with light!

LUDWIG. And when you molt, we'll make pillows!

JAMES. So dear Lord, if you want me to have her, if you want me to be happy ...

LUDWIG. I know you can't speak, I'm not even sure if you have feet, but if your answer is yes ...

LUDWIG and JAMES. Give me a sign!

LUDWIG. A miracle!

JAMES. I'm begging you!

LUDWIG and JAMES. Please please please please please please please please ... *(We hear gorgeous Wagnerian music. Both James and Ludwig hear it; they move to the music simultaneously, enraptured.)* Yes! *(As Ludwig leans in to kiss his swan, James grabs the crystal swan and runs offstage.)*

LUDWIG. *(Watching his swan exit.)* But where are you going? Didn't you hear the music? Didn't anyone? Is it just me?

QUEEN. *(From offstage.)* Ludwig!

LUDWIG. *(To the swan.)* Come back! I have breadcrumbs! *(As we hear a police siren wail, Ludwig runs out, pursuing the swan.)*

MARGARET. James. *(Lights up on the Avery parlor, in Texas. James is now lying on the floor, having just been severely beaten. Margaret Avery is standing over James. She is a young Texas matron, in a cheap but clean cotton dress. Margaret is James' mother; while she's concerned for his welfare, she's also short-tempered and strict.)* Not so smart now, are you, mister? Now that your daddy's beaten some sense into you.

JAMES. Bitch.

MARGARET. *(Margaret hauls off and smacks James very hard across the face.)* You watch your filthy mouth. This is the third time that I have had to go down to that police station, the third time that I have had to grovel and apologize, and the third time that I have had to live in shame, because my son is a filthy disgrace!

JAMES. I'm not your son.

MARGARET. I wish you weren't!

JAMES. I was switched at birth by gypsies. And they said, let's punish this baby. Let's send him to Dainsville, Texas, let's dump

10

him into a frame house with no books and brown wallpaper and pink chenille bedspreads ...

MARGARET. You spiteful little jabber-monster ...

JAMES. Let's give him to a sadistic idiot who runs a hardware store and a vicious, dried-up woman with bad hair and no taste.

MARGARET. *(Raising her hand.)* You are just begging for it ...

JAMES. Fine. Hit me again. But just look at your dining room.

MARGARET. But why? Why are you like this?

JAMES. Like what?

MARGARET. All I want is to help you. Don't you want to make your daddy proud?

JAMES. But my daddy gets drunk and he hits me. And sometimes he even hits you.

MARGARET. Not as hard.

SALLY. Mrs. Avery? *(Sally Mortimer enters. She is played by an adult actress, but she's currently ten years old. She is very pretty, very cheerful, and she's dressed in a crisp, frilly, almost Shirley Temple-style dress.)*

MARGARET. Come in. James, this is Sally Mortimer, whose family owns the department store.

SALLY. And I'm in the fourth grade, just like you.

MARGARET. And I have asked her to come here, so that you can apologize for your crime, to her face.

SALLY. *(Indicating that she'd like to be alone with James.)* Mrs. Avery?

MARGARET. Oh, of course. This is so sweet! *(Margaret exits.)*

SALLY. Now James, why did you steal that crystal swan?

JAMES. I didn't steal it. I needed it. Because it was beautiful.

SALLY. You mean, like a tree or a sunset?

JAMES. Or you.

SALLY. Well, that's no crime.

JAMES. You see?

SALLY. Now, why don't you kiss me, just right here on my cheek, and then all will be forgiven. *(Sally presents her cheek to be kissed. Just as James is about to kiss it, he kisses her lips instead.)* James! Why did you do that?

JAMES. I've got my eye on a punchbowl.

SALLY. Oh James, I know that deep down inside, you are really a very sweet, very good little boy.

JAMES. I'm a cocksucker.

SALLY. Well, that's fine. I'm a Baptist. *(Lights down on Texas, as Ludwig enters, now thirteen.)*

LUDWIG. I'm sorry! *(Queen Marie, Ludwig's mother, enters; she is played by the same actress who plays Margaret. The Queen loves her son deeply, but she is a fretful, deeply conventional woman. She also has very good reasons for her family concerns.)*

QUEEN. Ludwig! You're thirteen, a young man. Why are you acting like a spiteful, wretched little spoiled infant? Your father is furious.

LUDWIG. I don't care!

QUEEN. He's the king!

LUDWIG. I'm the prince!

QUEEN. I'm the queen!

LUDWIG. Gin!

QUEEN. Ludwig! Why did you fire that footman? He was the third one this month!

LUDWIG. I didn't want to, I didn't mean to. He was kind, he was clever.

QUEEN. Then why?

LUDWIG. *(Tormented.)* He was — ugly! *(Lights down on Bavaria. Lights up on a boy's bedroom in Texas. There is an open window and a bed with someone sleeping in it. The someone is Henry Lee Stafford, played by an adult actor but currently twelve years old. He wears pajamas. Henry Lee is a good-natured, trusting kid, anxious to do well, but he's far less sure of himself than James. Henry Lee has great promise, but he always tries to behave. James climbs into the bedroom through the window. The room is in semi-darkness. James now wears a Cub Scout uniform, including the cap and neckerchief. He carries a wrapped bundle.)*

JAMES. Henry Lee? *(Henry Lee wakes up, still groggy.)*

HENRY LEE. *(Scared.)* Who ... who is that? Who's there?

JAMES. It's me, James Avery.

HENRY LEE. *What are you doing here?*

JAMES. I've seen you at school, in gym class. You were looking at me.

HENRY LEE. I was not!

JAMES. Do you want to have sex?

HENRY LEE. *What?*

JAMES. Now that I'm twelve, I have it all the time.

HENRY LEE. With who?

JAMES. Me.

HENRY LEE. Get out of my house! I'm gonna yell! *(James jumps onto the bed and yanks Henry Lee's hand behind his back; he covers Henry Lee's mouth with his other hand.)*

JAMES. *(Gleeful.)* Don't make me kiss you. *(Henry Lee bites James' hand and James yells.)* Shit! You bit me! You fight like a girl!

HENRY LEE. I do not!

JAMES. It was a compliment!

HENRY LEE. Get off my bed! Get out of my house!

JAMES. Do you wanna see what I use, for sex?

HENRY LEE. What?

JAMES. *(Holding up the bundle.)* Look.

HENRY LEE. What is that?

JAMES. *(Taking a large art book out of the bundle.)* I got this from the library this afternoon. From the special adult section, behind the front desk.

HENRY LEE. But we're not supposed to go back there.

JAMES. I hid in the bathroom until the librarian went out, and then I grabbed it. It burned my hands.

HENRY LEE. Why?

JAMES. Because when a book is forbidden and sick and evil, when it's in the adult section, it has special, dark powers. Do you know what they call those books?

HENRY LEE. What?

JAMES. Bestsellers.

HENRY LEE. *(Impressed.)* Really?

JAMES. So I dropped it out the window, and then I ran outside and I picked it up.

HENRY LEE. You stole it.

JAMES. I needed it.

HENRY LEE. What's the difference?

JAMES. What do you want, more than anything else in the whole entire world?

HENRY LEE. I want — to make my parents and my teachers and everyone else in Dainsville really proud of me.

JAMES. I love that.

HENRY LEE. You do?

JAMES. So you wanna be an asshole.

HENRY LEE. No!

JAMES. But what do you *need*, in your soul?

HENRY LEE. A Cadillac.

JAMES. Yeah!

HENRY LEE. A midnight-blue convertible, like in that Cary Grant movie, with whitewall tires and real leather seats and all that chrome.

JAMES. Baby!

HENRY LEE. I need it whenever my Little League coach says that the whole team is depending on me. Or when my mom says that "a B-plus is unacceptable." *(Grabbing James around the throat, acting it out.)* I need it when my dad holds a sawed-off shotgun to my head and says, "Boy, if you don't get into Texas A&M, I'm gonna splatter your brains all over the kitchen wall." *(Really going wild.)* But then I grab the gun, and I blast *his* head off, and I blast every window and trophy and piece of fine china in the house! And I set the whole place on fire and I climb out on the roof and I yell, "Come and get me, coppers!"

JAMES. Henry Lee.

HENRY LEE. Yeah?

JAMES. Not the china.

HENRY LEE. Okay.

JAMES. So if we were just walking down the street and we just happened to pass a midnight-blue Cadillac, and the keys were in the ignition and the radio is playing a great song ...

HENRY LEE. Like Benny Goodman ...

JAMES. Or Tommy Dorsey ...

HENRY LEE. Or like, the Andrews Sisters ...

JAMES. Which one's your favorite?

HENRY LEE. Patti. The pretty one.

JAMES. Me too. *(Very macho.)* Do you know what I'd like to do with her? Do you know what she needs?

HENRY LEE. What?

JAMES. *(Equally macho.)* A solo album.

HENRY LEE. *(Still macho.)* For damn sure!

JAMES. So if you walked past this Cadillac, and it sang to you, so if we took it out for a spin, like to Dallas or Hollywood or Mars, then what would you call that?

HENRY LEE. A dream.

JAMES. Now you're talkin'.

HENRY LEE. A bold escape!

JAMES. Together!

HENRY LEE. A crime.

JAMES. Even better!

HENRY LEE. Get out of my room!

JAMES. Look. *(He points a flashlight at the cover of the art book.)*

HENRY LEE. *(Reading the title.)* The History of Greco-Roman Art.

JAMES. But I have to warn you. This book is completely filled with sex. It's oozing with sex. If you even look at one inch of one page, do you know what will happen to you?

HENRY LEE. What?

JAMES. Sex.

HENRY LEE. Stop it!

JAMES. Are you ready? Are you man enough?

HENRY LEE. *(After a beat.)* Yes. *(James points the beam of the flash-light at the book. As he slowly and dramatically opens the cover, we hear:)*

LUDWIG. But I can't! *(The flashlight goes out, as the lights come up instantly on the palace. Ludwig is standing, facing out. The Queen stands nearby. A uniformed footman, with a powdered wig and a some-what bloated body, stands facing Ludwig, with his back to the audience — we will never see the footman's face. Ludwig, in his reaction to the footman, is not being deliberately mean or cruel. His aesthetic drive is helpless; he can't control his visceral sense of taste. He's in torment.)*

QUEEN. But you must. I want you to stare directly at this foot-man, for a period of no less than one hour.

LUDWIG. An *hour? (Appalled.)*

QUEEN. You can do it. I know you can.

LUDWIG. But — without breaks?

QUEEN. Your father insists.

LUDWIG. But he's grotesque.

QUEEN. He's still your father.

LUDWIG. *(Gesturing to the footman.)* I meant him. He's vile. He's repulsive.

QUEEN. Ludwig!

LUDWIG. *(Sincerely, to the footman.)* No offense.

QUEEN. Darling, one day you're going to be king, of all Bavarians, not just the cute ones. *(Ludwig starts to run.)* Come back here!

LUDWIG. But I have this terrible problem, and I know it's com-pletely my fault, but when I see something — not beautiful, when it's drab and misshapen, when it's — what's the word?

QUEEN. English?

LUDWIG. Yes! I have a physical reaction, a spasm, I can't control it.

QUEEN. You must try.

LUDWIG. I want to, I need to, but I'm frightened.

QUEEN. *(Holding a pocket watch.)* Let's begin. *(Ludwig steels himself; he stares at the footman's face. Blackout on the palace. The flashlight beam appears, illuminating the book, as James and Henry Lee sit on the bed, poring over the pages.)*

HENRY LEE. Oh my God …

JAMES. *(Turning a page.)* And this one …

HENRY LEE. Look at that.

JAMES. *(Turning the page.)* And two of them!

HENRY LEE. But, but — they're naked. All of the statues. You can see — everything.

JAMES. Of course. This was B.C.

HENRY LEE. B.C.?

JAMES. Before Clothes.

HENRY LEE. Shut up!

JAMES. But why is that guy so big and built, but his dickie is so tiny?

HENRY LEE. You're already bigger than he is.

JAMES. So you looked.

HENRY LEE. I did not!

JAMES. And when I get a boner, it gets even bigger. Do you know why?

HENRY LEE. Why?

JAMES. I'm an American.

HENRY LEE. What are you doing?

JAMES. I'm touching myself.

HENRY LEE. Why?

JAMES. It's like, if I see something, or someone, really beautiful, my hand goes right there, like a compass.

HENRY LEE. But my dickie is so hard! It hurts!

JAMES. So touch it. Play with it.

HENRY LEE. But it's wrong. It's dirty.

JAMES. It's beautiful. It says so, right in the Bible.

HENRY LEE. Where?

JAMES. In Ezekiel 12. God says, "Ezekiel, you're twelve. Touch yourself."

HENRY LEE. *(Putting his hand inside his pajamas.)* Thy will be done …

JAMES. Look at me.

HENRY LEE. Why?

JAMES. I'm Hercules.

HENRY LEE. I'm Apollo.

JAMES. I'm a gladiator.

HENRY LEE. I'm glad.

JAMES. We're wrestling …

HENRY LEE. In the Colosseum …

JAMES. In the Olympics …

HENRY LEE. In the nude …

JAMES. Yes!

QUEEN. *(Consulting her pocket watch.)* Thirty-seven minutes …

LUDWIG. *(To the footman, feverishly.)* I'm trying to love you, to be a good king, but it's hard. But you're helping me, I can feel it, to appreciate all kinds of beauty, it's growing, it's blossoming, a whole new concept, I love your ears, I love your eyes, I love your — were you in an accident?

HENRY LEE. The whole Colosseum is on its feet, they're all watching the two gladiators ...

JAMES. The slaves are watching ...

HENRY LEE. And the citizens ...

JAMES. And the Emperor ...

HENRY LEE. Hi, everybody!

JAMES. They're all cheering ...

HENRY LEE. They're all chanting ...

JAMES and HENRY LEE. Go, go, go ...

QUEEN. Forty-eight minutes! You're doing great!

LUDWIG. I can't! I can't! Not one second more!

QUEEN. I have faith! Keep looking! Go, go, go ...

QUEEN, JAMES and HENRY LEE. Go, go, go, go, go, go, go ...

LUDWIG. *(Over the go, go, go's:)* But my eyes are on fire! They're going to pop out!

JAMES. It's happening! In front of everyone! We're gonna spurt!

HENRY LEE. We're gonna shoot!

QUEEN. Fifty-eight minutes ...

JAMES. All over each other and the Emperor and the Acropolis!

HENRY LEE. This is the best book I've ever read!

QUEEN. We're almost there!

JAMES, HENRY LEE and LUDWIG. *(James and Henry Lee are coming, noisily, while Ludwig is crying out:)* AHHH!

QUEEN. One hour! Congratulations!

LUDWIG. But I can't do this! I can't be king!

QUEEN. *(Embracing him.)* Of course you can. And you're going to be the most wonderful king.

LUDWIG. Really, Mummy?

QUEEN. Of course. And next time you'll do even better.

LUDWIG. Next time? What do you mean?

QUEEN. *(To the footman.)* Bring in your wife.

LUDWIG. NO! *(As Ludwig runs out, lights down on the palace.)*

HENRY LEE. James?

JAMES. Yeah?

HENRY LEE. What ... what just happened? What did we do?

JAMES. I think that, for maybe one hot second, that we both — left Texas.

17

HENRY LEE. We did?

JAMES. Swear.

HENRY LEE. What?

JAMES. Swear that we will go all the way.

HENRY LEE. What do you mean?

JAMES. Swear that someday, when we get bigger, the minute we can — that we will get the hell out of here. All the way.

HENRY LEE. To where?

JAMES. To out there. To happiness. To someplace so beautiful it gives you a boner.

HENRY LEE. But why me?

JAMES. Because I look at everybody in this town. I stare at 'em.

HENRY LEE. Like a hobby?

JAMES. To try and see what's beautiful about them. What they dream about. Who they love. But most people, they look away. They don't want me to know. But you looked right back.

HENRY LEE. And it scared me. It was like in *Superman*, when he uses his X-ray vision, and it starts a fire.

JAMES. Just by lookin' at you, I can make your dickie hard. *(James stares at Henry Lee, in the eyes.)*

HENRY LEE. Oh my God! And that was so fast!

JAMES. We're twelve.

HENRY LEE. James!

JAMES. You are the best little boy in Dainsville. And I'm the worst. If we get together, we could explode!

HENRY LEE. Right out of Texas! *(James grabs the art book and holds it out.)*

JAMES. Do you swear? You and me? All the way? Look at me.

HENRY LEE. But if I look at you, I'll say yes.

JAMES. I know.

HENRY LEE. *(Looking right at him.)* Yes. *(Lights out on Henry Lee's bedroom, as Ludwig sweeps onstage, dressed in a full, billowing nun's habit and wimple. He faces the audience, kneels and crosses himself in prayer.)*

LUDWIG. Dear Heavenly Father, Today I am fourteen years old, and I am in desperate need. So I have decided to speak to you most humbly, dressed in the habit of your most sainted and elegant creatures. To purify myself completely, for the past two weeks I have fasted. I have taken absolutely no sustenance, except dessert.

OTTO. *(From offstage.)* Ludwig!

LUDWIG. *(To God.)* My little brother, Otto.

OTTO. *(From offstage.)* Luddy!

LUDWIG. *(To God.)* One day, when my father dies, I will become king. So I need to know: When the time comes, how can I make the world as beautiful as You? *(Otto, Ludwig's seven-year-old brother, enters, played by the same adult actor who will later play Pfeiffer. He wears lederhosen and a cap, and carries a rubber ball. He is sweet-natured but far less sophisticated than Ludwig.)*

OTTO. Luddy!

LUDWIG. I'm talking to God!

OTTO. But I want to play! Please, Luddy!

LUDWIG. What did you call me?

OTTO. Luddy! Luddy, Luddy, Luddy!

LUDWIG. *(To God.)* Dear Lord, I seek guidance … *(Listening to God's advice.)* Yes … yes … I'll tell him.

OTTO. What did God say?

LUDWIG. God says that he wants to see you. Right *now. (Ludwig chases Otto, who screams.)*

OTTO. No! Stop it! God didn't say that!

LUDWIG. Say it! Say what you're supposed to say!

OTTO. *(As Ludwig grabs Otto and starts to strangle him.)* Stop it! Mama! *(As Ludwig strangles Otto, the Queen rushes in and separates the boys.)*

QUEEN. Ludwig! Stop it! This instant! *(Ludwig reluctantly releases Otto, who lies on the ground, panting.)* You are dressed like a nun!

LUDWIG. I know that!

QUEEN. Then act like one!

OTTO. That's right!

QUEEN. What were you doing?

LUDWIG. I'm trying to learn to be king, but he wouldn't call me by my title!

OTTO. So he killed me!

QUEEN. Do you know what happens to bad little princes?

LUDWIG. What?

QUEEN. You'll end up — like your grandfather.

LUDWIG. How?

QUEEN. When he was king, he became obsessed with Lola Montes, a notorious courtesan. A courtesan — do you know what that is?

LUDWIG. No.

QUEEN. Good. She was an Irish girl, pretending to be an Arabian dancer. She would make a movement with her hips, which would drive men into a filthy, deranged erotic frenzy.

LUDWIG. What was it? *(The Queen, after a moment's preparation, demonstrates the hip-swivelling movement.)* That's it?

QUEEN. She had lighting.

LUDWIG. And Grandfather?

QUEEN. He ran off with Lola, and the nation was outraged. He refused to give her up, he spent millions, and finally — he was forced to do something horrible. Something unthinkable. Something that no king, of any country, should ever, ever have to do.

LUDWIG. *(Sincerely, shocked.)* His own laundry?

QUEEN. He was forced to leave the throne. To abdicate. In *disgrace.*

LUDWIG and OTTO. No!

QUEEN. Your father has grown very preoccupied, so your future has become entirely my domain. And I'm a normal woman. All I want is for this family to be happy and healthy and to rule Bavaria. Is that too much to ask?

LUDWIG. No, Mummy.

QUEEN. Without any hint of scandal, excess or perversion.

OTTO. Mummy, what's perversion?

QUEEN. It's a Latin term.

OTTO. For what?

QUEEN. Your brother.

LUDWIG. How dare you!

OTTO. You see? Luddy is snooty, because he's going to be king!

QUEEN. *(To Otto.)* But sweetheart, you're just as important, in case Ludwig gets assassinated, commits suicide or goes mad.

OTTO. Really?

QUEEN. You're the spare.

LUDWIG. Mummy!

QUEEN. But that won't happen, not if we all love each other and pull together and wear men's clothing. Do you understand me, Ludwig?

LUDWIG. Yes, Mummy.

QUEEN. So what are you going to do? *(Ludwig, apprehensive but determined, takes off his nun's habit. He stands in his long underwear, which has a royal crest embroidered on the chest. Ludwig is reluctant to remove his wimple.)* And? *(Ludwig removes his wimple.)* Much better.

LUDWIG. But I feel so — naked. And cold. No, worse than that, much worse, I feel — ordinary. Invisible. How will God find me?

QUEEN. He'll find you because He loves you.

LUDWIG. *(Longingly.)* Just the wimple?

QUEEN. No. Now Otto, what's your brother's title?

OTTO. Your Highness.

QUEEN. That's my good boy. And Ludwig, who are you going to be?

LUDWIG. *(Proudly.)* The king.

OTTO. Of my butt.

LUDWIG. Otto! *(Ludwig chases him offstage, as Otto screams.)*

QUEEN. Boys! *(As she pursues the boys.)* I am serious! *(As the Queen exits after her sons, we hear a police siren wail. James appears, standing behind bars, in handcuffs. His clothing and hair are disheveled. Sally Mortimer, now fifteen, runs onstage, very excited. She carries a plate of freshly baked cookies.)*

SALLY. James! Is it true?

JAMES. What?

SALLY. I can scarcely even speak the words. They said, I heard — that you ran off with Henry Lee Stafford.

JAMES. Yes I did!

SALLY. And that before you left Dainsville, you set fire to your family's home.

JAMES. It was so great. It was my fifteenth birthday, and my father beat the hell out of me. So I asked, now, Daddy, what was that for? And he said, "Happy birthday, you little faggot."

SALLY. Oh no!

JAMES. That's right.

SALLY. Was there cake?

JAMES. No. *(Sally gasps.)* But then I thought, maybe he's right. So I asked myself, now just what would a little faggot do?

SALLY. So you burned down your house?

JAMES. I redecorated.

SALLY. And then they caught you and Henry Lee, five miles outside of town, in a stolen pickup truck.

JAMES. You know it!

SALLY. But *why?*

JAMES. We couldn't find a Cadillac.

SALLY. James!

JAMES. We were flyin', we were gone!

SALLY. Where?

JAMES. To some place so beautiful, you can't even imagine it!

SALLY. The state capitol?

JAMES. Picture it, Sally, like if you were with us. We're hittin' eighty miles an hour, the windows wide open, your hair shootin' straight back …

SALLY. Oh my Lord ...

JAMES. I mean, we felt like we could be anybody we wanted!

SALLY. Anybody?

JAMES. Who would you be?

SALLY. I would be ... I would be ... I would be me. And I'd stay home.

JAMES. Why?

SALLY. Because I'm popular. Do you realize how many valentines I received, this year alone? So many that I actually gave several of them to Emmeline Atwood, that sweet, brave, wonderful girl, who's blind? I just put them on her desk and I said ... *(Raising her voice.)* "Emmeline, these are for you!"

JAMES. Did she like them?

SALLY. Especially the embossed ones.

JAMES. What are you doing here? In the police station?

SALLY. I came because I heard that your parents refuse to see you, and that you are being sent away, and that Henry Lee's parents insist that he was a hostage.

JAMES. A hostage?

SALLY. Did you hypnotize him, did you drug him with opium, were you going to sell him to bloodthirsty Chinese pirates as a helpless white slave?

JAMES. Later.

SALLY. I knew it!

JAMES. What are you doing here?

SALLY. I came because no one else would. I came out of goodness and mercy. Ginger snap? *(She begins to feed James cookies, through the bars.)*

JAMES. My favorite. You know why?

SALLY. Because they're tasty yet not all that fattening?

JAMES. Before I bite one, I like to lick it, with my tongue. *(As James licks a cookie, erotically:)*

SALLY. James — that is no way to treat a cookie.

JAMES. You came because you like me.

SALLY. I did not!

JAMES. You came because I once saw your notebook, in geometry class. And you were drawing a picture of me.

SALLY. That was a trapezoid.

JAMES. With my eyes?

SALLY. But I couldn't really get them. Your eyes are so wicked. Like they can see — everything.

JAMES. I can see beneath your clothes right now. You are wearing very clean underwear.

SALLY. That's incredible!

JAMES. And your nipples are hard.

SALLY. It's January!

JAMES. Sally, could you just kind of sneak into the sheriff's office, and kind of grab the keys? *(Indicating the handcuffs.)*

SALLY. Absolutely not! That is illegal!

JAMES. I fucked Henry Lee.

SALLY. James!

JAMES. Well, not yet. He's stubborn.

SALLY. I am leaving!

JAMES. No, please, just stay one more second, just turn around and let me look at you. You are so good and so pretty, you are the prettiest girl in Dainsville. *(Sally pauses and turns, so that James can see her.)*

SALLY. Just for one second. And I am only doing this as an act of charity. Sometimes, when Emmeline gets depressed, I describe myself.

JAMES. While I'm away, will you write to me?

SALLY. I just don't know.

JAMES. Will you pray for me?

SALLY. I will try.

JAMES. And the very first time that you have sex, whenever and wherever, will you call out my name?

SALLY. James Avery! I have tried to help you, to show you some simple human compassion, but everyone is right! You don't deserve cookies!

JAMES. Will you?

SALLY. *(On her way out.)* Yes. *(Sally exits, as James smiles. Lights down on James, as we hear the sound of metal doors clanging shut, followed by a Wagnerian trill. Helmut jogs onstage; he is Ludwig's fitness instructor. He is a handsome, well-built, very energetic fellow, determined to inspire his students. Helmut might have a German, almost Schwarzenegger accent. He is played by the same actor who plays Henry Lee.)*

HELMUT. Five more miles! *(Ludwig, now sixteen, staggers onstage, wearing a long sleeved knit shirt and bloomers, his workout attire.)*

LUDWIG. Are you mad?

HELMUT. Your Highness, I am your fitness instructor. And your parents insist — you need a full program of rigorous exercise.

LUDWIG. But why?

HELMUT. You're sixteen years old, and we must channel your physical urges.

23

LUDWIG. My urges? For what?

HELMUT. Don't you know?

LUDWIG. I've been kept in the castle since birth. No one tells me anything.

HELMUT. I'll tell you. But first — we shall wrestle.

LUDWIG. But what about my urges?

HELMUT. As we compete! *(Ludwig gets on all fours. Helmut kneels beside him.)* Wrestle!

LUDWIG. Stop, I'm not ready, I should wrestle someone smaller, someone crippled, someone dead ...

HELMUT. And down! *(Helmut slams Ludwig onto his stomach and lies on top of him.)*

LUDWIG. I can't breathe ...

HELMUT. Hormones. When a boy becomes a man, the blood surges through his body, moving directly to his groin. And when he sees a beautiful young lady, alluringly attired ...

LUDWIG. In say, pale yellow crepe du chine ...

HELMUT. Her lively eyes sparkle, her luscious bosom heaves ...

LUDWIG. In her low-cut bodice, in the style of the Empress Josephine ...

HELMUT. His young heart pounds, his savage mind burns scarlet, when he gazes at her he can think of one thing and one thing only ...

LUDWIG. Yes!

HELMUT. What?

LUDWIG. The perfect hat!

HELMUT. No! Again! *(Helmut gets on all fours, and Ludwig kneels beside him.)* Put one hand on my forearm, and the other around my waist. *(Ludwig does this.)*

LUDWIG. Helmut, I have been noticing changes. I have gained fifteen pounds, my voice has deepened, and I can now grow a full moustache.

HELMUT. Exactly!

LUDWIG. I am more like my mother every day.

HELMUT. No. Your Highness, have you ever seen a naked woman?

LUDWIG. In my books of mythology.

HELMUT. Good. So let us say that Zeus, he comes upon Aphrodite, lying nude in a secluded forest glade.

LUDWIG. Near Olympus ...

HELMUT. Her flesh is moist, his desire mounts ...

LUDWIG. Cupid hovers nearby ...

HELMUT. Try to pin me! *(Helmut remains stationary, on all fours, while Ludwig climbs all over him, trying vainly to pin him. As they wrestle:)*

LUDWIG. But what happens with Zeus? What do they do?

HELMUT. Pretend I'm Aphrodite! I'm teasing you!

LUDWIG. You little goddess!

HELMUT. Capture me, Your Majesty! Ravish me!

LUDWIG. Here I come!

HELMUT. Oh Your Highness, you overpower me! *(Helmut flips over, allowing himself to be pinned, pulling Ludwig on top of him.)*

LUDWIG. You let me do that!

HELMUT. As will your bride. She'll say yes, Your Highness, plunge your fine silver dagger into my trembling satin pillow.

LUDWIG. Helmut?

HELMUT. Thrust your shining strong rapier into my ripe pomegranate.

LUDWIG. I'm not following …

HELMUT. These are metaphors — put your penis into her vagina.

LUDWIG. I like metaphors.

HELMUT. Is it clear, what will be expected?

LUDWIG. I'm more confused than ever. Helmut, are you in love?

HELMUT. Your Highness!

LUDWIG. Are you?

HELMUT. Well, yes. With my Hilda.

LUDWIG. Hilda! Helmut and Hilda!

HELMUT. It sounds pretty.

LUDWIG. Like a puppet show. Is it like in the stories? Like Elsa and Lohengrin?

HELMUT. Lohengrin?

LUDWIG. It's my very favorite legend. Elsa is the innocent maiden, and Lohengrin is a magical knight who appears and saves her. Is it opera?

HELMUT. Why opera?

LUDWIG. That's the test. If your love is truly miraculous, then it rises, it breaks free, it becomes music. So what you've been trying to tell me, about these urges, when you're with your Hilda, do you sing?

HELMUT. Sing? No!

LUDWIG. But this is what terrifies me. That I'll do all that is expected and yet — I'll be alone. Forever. In silence.

HELMUT. But that doesn't have to happen. You can be so happy. I will show you, what men and women do together. *(Helmut grabs Ludwig and kisses him passionately.)* There! Isn't that wonderful?

And now let us strip off our clothes and leap into the river! *(Helmut runs offstage, taking off his clothes. Ludwig, still reeling from the kiss, tries to sing, in a small, strangled yet joyously ardent voice.)*

LUDWIG. *(Singing.)* La!

HELMUT. *(From offstage.)* Your Highness! *(Ludwig runs offstage, after Helmut. As Ludwig runs out, we hear the sound of rushing water. Lights up on the Dainsville High School boys' locker room, including at least one locker and a bench. We hear the sounds of guys leaving the locker room, laughing and shouting. Henry Lee, now eighteen, enters, naked except for a towel wrapped around his waist. As he approaches his locker, James steps out from behind the locker. James is now also eighteen, and he wears jeans and a T-shirt. There's a swagger to him; he's grown up a.lot faster and rougher than the other teenagers in Dainsville.)*

JAMES. You win?

HENRY LEE. 'Scuse me? Oh my God.

JAMES. Look at you.

HENRY LEE. James? Avery?

JAMES. Henry Lee Stafford, all grown up.

HENRY LEE. I thought — aren't you in reform school?

JAMES. I'm out. A proud graduate. *(Staring at Henry Lee.)* Baby. Three whole years.

HENRY LEE. But what are you doing here?

JAMES. I came back.

HENRY LEE. Why?

JAMES. One reason.

HENRY LEE. What?

JAMES. You. *(We hear offstage voices calling out, "Hank, come on! We're goin'!" Etc.)*

HENRY LEE. *(Calling out.)* Go on ahead, you guys! — I'll catch up! James, I'm getting dressed, could you please go outside?

JAMES. But I have so much to tell you. Reform school was the best. Now I can get into a really good prison.

HENRY LEE. James …

JAMES. Man, it is so good to see you …

HENRY LEE. James?

JAMES. Yeah?

HENRY LEE. James, a lot has happened since you went away. I've changed. I've shaped up.

JAMES. Nice work. Greco-Roman.

HENRY LEE. Okay, look, I know you've had a bad deal, and I'd like to help you, but I have to get dressed, I have to meet Sally.

JAMES. Sally?

HENRY LEE. Sally Mortimer.

JAMES. Henry Lee — this is James.

HENRY LEE. So what? What's that supposed to mean?

JAMES. I got tattooed, at Laredo.

HENRY LEE. How?

JAMES. With a candle, a razor blade and a ballpoint pen. *(James rolls up his sleeve, revealing a crude tattoo.)*

HENRY LEE. *(Reading the tattoo, stunned.)* "Henry Lee." Oh my God.

JAMES. And it hurt, like a son-of-a-bitch. So I screamed and I spat and I cursed you.

HENRY LEE. Why?

JAMES. Because you have two names.

HENRY LEE. Get out. Right now. Your parents and this town sent you away for a very good reason, but I don't think it helped.

JAMES. But this will. *(James reaches out and grabs Henry Lee's towel.)*

HENRY LEE. Give that back!

JAMES. *(Calling out.)* Help me, someone! Henry Lee Stafford is exposing himself!

HENRY LEE. *(Calling out.)* No I'm not!

JAMES. I can't look! But I will!

HENRY LEE. You don't know what it was like! *(Henry Lee goes to the locker, and starts putting on his clothes.)*

JAMES. When?

HENRY LEE. After you left! Everyone was watching me, every minute, they thought I was — you!

JAMES. Me?

HENRY LEE. But I showed them. I showed everyone.

JAMES. What?

HENRY LEE. *(He takes a football out of his locker; he is now dangerously angry.)* This. *(Henry Lee throws the football very hard and fast, right at James.)*

JAMES. Watch it!

HENRY LEE. Do you know who I am? Do you have any idea?

JAMES. Who?

HENRY LEE. I am the captain and the starting quarterback of the Dainsville Dynamos. I am president of the senior class, the Honor Society, the debate team and the Junior Chamber of Commerce Young Texas Achievers.

JAMES. Why?

HENRY LEE. Because you're not. Because I was voted Most Popular, Smartest, Most Athletic and Most Likely To Succeed.

JAMES. What about Best Looking?

HENRY LEE. I turned it down.

JAMES. Why?

HENRY LEE. Most Modest.

JAMES. But what about your criminal record? Your evil past?

HENRY LEE. Fine, I admit it. Like a million years ago, we ... we ...

JAMES. Messed around?

HENRY LEE. But the whole time, I always used to pretend that you were a girl.

JAMES. And I pretended that you were a girl.

HENRY LEE. So it was perfectly normal.

JAMES. If we were lesbians.

HENRY LEE. No!

JAMES. We stole a truck! We tried to run away together!

HENRY LEE. I was a hostage!

JAMES. You — *drove!*

HENRY LEE. So?

JAMES. You are so beautiful.

HENRY LEE. Guys aren't beautiful!

JAMES. You are. Kiss me.

HENRY LEE. No!

JAMES. Fuck me.

HENRY LEE. Get away from me!

JAMES. Hit me.

HENRY LEE. What?

JAMES. If you won't kiss me or, fuck me, then hit me. Because it's the only way you're gonna stop me. Hit me!

HENRY LEE. I won't! I'm a Christian!

JAMES. I'm not. Here I come! *(Henry Lee slugs James, who crumples.)*

HENRY LEE. I'm sorry, but you asked for it, you had it comin'. *(As James remains doubled over. James whimpers.)* Are you okay? *(James pops up, unhurt. He gleefully slugs Henry Lee. Henry Lee crumples.)* Where'd you learn to do that?

JAMES. Recess. *(Henry Lee slugs James, who hits him back. As they fight:)* This is great! This is hot! This is the way Texans have sex!

HENRY LEE. You are disgusting. You are exactly the same.

JAMES. No I'm not. I'm even better at it. I've had lots of time to think about my crimes and my sins and my tendencies. And do you know what I've decided? I love them. They are the very best part of me. And they are gonna save me.

HENRY LEE. They'll destroy you.

JAMES. Henry Lee, I know it's been forever, and I know that your folks and this town and this world have slammed down on you, but that's all over. They can't stop us, not anymore. Look at me.

HENRY LEE. I can't. I can't let my eyes do that. Not anymore.

JAMES. But why not?

HENRY LEE. Because I am getting married. Tomorrow.

JAMES. To who?

HENRY LEE. To Sally.

JAMES. Do you love her?

HENRY LEE. She's so pretty, you should see her ...

JAMES. Do you love her?

HENRY LEE. Her father owns the department store, I have a future there ...

JAMES. Do you love her?

HENRY LEE. Yes. *(Ludwig runs onstage. Lights down on the locker room.)*

LUDWIG. I can't do this. It's insane. It's unnatural. *(The Queen enters.)*

QUEEN. It's exciting! You're seventeen, and you get to choose a bride!

LUDWIG. But I need to fall in love!

QUEEN. And you shall. I have hired the most extraordinary man to help with our plans — our new deputy secretary, Johannes Pfeiffer. He's been employed by the royal families of Normandy, Norway, Madrid and Milan. *(Johannes Pfeiffer enters. He is a dignified, perfectly groomed gentleman, wearing an immaculate uniform. He is a superb diplomat; he prides himself on his perfect posture, his ability to instill discipline and his comprehensive knowledge of human affairs.)*

PFEIFFER. *Bonjour. Guten Morgen. Buenas dias.*

QUEEN. *(Delighted.)* Your first task is to find Ludwig a bride.

PFEIFFER. *Arrivederci. (Pfeiffer starts to exit.)*

QUEEN. No! He needs to produce an heir to the throne!

LUDWIG. An *heir?*

PFEIFFER. Very well. May I present our first candidate for royal matrimony — Princess Patricia, of Prussia! *(We hear a regal trumpet flourish, and Princess Patricia, a young beauty, enters, in a ballgown and a tiara. She is poised and gracious, and speaks with a demure German accent. She will be played by the same actress who plays Sally. Pfeiffer and the Queen exit.)*

PATRICIA. *(Curtsying.)* Your Highness.

29

LUDWIG. Good morning,

PATRICIA. I know zis is awkvard, but I'd weally like to get to know you, as a person.

LUDWIG. That's — very nice.

PATRICIA. I only haf vun possible dwawback.

LUDWIG. Yes?

PATRICIA. Vell, to keep our bloodlines pure, most of my ancestors mawwied zere cousins. Who mawwied zere cousins and so on, for over 2,000 years. So by now, my family has become, well ...

LUDWIG. Odd? Eccentric?

PATRICIA. Unique. My gweat-aunt, Empwess Cowinthia of Portugal, vas born mute. Shall I do my impwession of her?

LUDWIG. Your impwession? *(Patricia turns away for a moment, to prepare. Then she faces Ludwig and mouths the word "Hello," silently.)* Bwavo.

PATRICIA. And my uncle, Duke Ferdinand of Finland, he has blue eyes.

LUDWIG. So?

PATRICIA. For lunch.

LUDWIG. Ah.

PATRICIA. And my dearest sister, Pwincess Penelope, is convinced that she is actually a gwand piano.

LUDWIG. But how tragic.

PATRICIA. Not at parties.

LUDWIG. Next!

PATRICIA. Pwincess Enid, of England. *(Patricia exits, and with another trumpet flourish, Princess Enid enters. She will be played by the same actress who plays the Queen. She wears formal riding clothes. She has an English accent and a jolly, chummy, gung-ho quality.)*

ENID. Hallo, Ludwig!

LUDWIG. Hello?

ENID. I've heard so much about you. I think we'd make a marvelous match.

LUDWIG. I can't do this ...

ENID. But why not?

LUDWIG. You — you remind me of my mother.

ENID. But how lucky!

LUDWIG. Lucky?

ENID. Every fellow secretly yearns to marry his mother.

LUDWIG. Why?

ENID. You can return to childhood, to the womb. Just imagine, getting chummy with your mummy ... *(She links arms with Ludwig.)*

LUDWIG. Chummy?

ENID. Feeling plummy with your mummy ...

LUDWIG. Plummy?

ENID. Let your mummy rub your tummy ...

LUDWIG. Stop it!

ENID. *(As she caresses him.)* Don't get glummy with your mummy, just succumb-y to your mummy, put your thumbie in your mummy ...

LUDWIG. *(Leaping up.)* No!

ENID. *(Threatening.)* Don't play dummy with your mummy!

LUDWIG. Next!

ENID. Princess Ursula the Unusual, of Albania! *(Princess Enid exits, as Princess Ursula enters, with another trumpet flourish. She is played by the same actor who plays Pfeiffer. She wears a tiara atop a wig of sausage curls, and a hoop-skirted ballgown. Ursula is girlishly shy, flirtatious and deeply virginal. She carries a fan, and speaks in a high, feminine tone.)*

URSULA. Hello, Ludwig.

LUDWIG. Enid, come back!

URSULA. I am not like the other girls.

LUDWIG. Oh no?

URSULA. But the nuns, at my convent school, they tell me I am beautiful.

LUDWIG. They're nuns.

URSULA. In Albania, they have a name for a girl such as I.

LUDWIG. "The big girl"?

URSULA. Oh, no.

LUDWIG. "The tall girl"?

URSULA. No again.

LUDWIG. "The goalie"?

URSULA. It's true! You see, I possess the sexual organs of both genders. Isn't that marvelous?

LUDWIG. You're a date.

URSULA. *(Very sweet and feminine.)* I'll kiss you and caress you.

LUDWIG. And then?

URSULA. *(Dropping her voice, to a rugged, threatening bass, very macho.)* I'll fuck you raw.

LUDWIG. Next! *(As Ludwig exits, Ursula steps forward.)*

URSULA. And now the greatest princess of them all, in her bedroom, the seventeen-year-old Sally Mortimer, of Dainsville, Texas.

(Ursula exits. Lights up on Sally, now seventeen, wearing a pretty, frilly bathrobe, seated before her vanity table, facing the audience. A deluxe, full-length wedding gown is worn by a dressmaking mannequin which stands nearby. As Sally speaks to the audience, she might brush her hair and apply makeup. Sally's tone during this speech should never be bitchy or condescending. It's her wedding day, and she's on a sincere spiritual quest.)

SALLY. Some people think that I had — feelings for James Avery, but that is just not true. But before he — went away, he always used to say something which I will never forget. He would say that he'd been studying the situation since kindergarten, and that he'd made lists and charts and held a personal pageant, and that he had finally determined that I was the prettiest girl in all of Dainsville. And he said that the prettiest girl can give people hope, and brighten their day, and wasn't that just a wonderful thing to say? Especially for a delinquent? And ever since then, whenever I look in the mirror, I see Eleanor Roosevelt. Only, of course, pretty. I mean, Mrs. Roosevelt works so hard, trying to help the poor and the downtrodden, but can you imagine how much more she could do, if she were pretty? And of course, there's also inner beauty, but inner beauty is tricky, because you can't prove it. I've thought a lot about this, you know, about beauty and goodness, and all the different religions? I mean, Buddha is chubby — face it. And Confucius was all old and scraggly and, I imagine, single. And you're not even allowed to have a picture of Mohammed — was it the teeth? I don't know. But Jesus is always really pretty, with perfect skin and shiny hair, it's like God was saying, look to Jesus, for tips. But I know there's that German man, Adolf Hitler, and he thinks that everyone should be perfect and blue-eyed and beautiful, but that's wrong too, because then who would be the best friends? And I don't want to be vain or prideful, so I always remember what James said, in one of his letters. He said that there are only two things which really matter in life: youth and beauty. *(James enters, dressed as he was in the locker room. He is on the prowl, stalking Sally. She's frightened, nervous and very drawn to James.)*

JAMES. *Truth* and beauty.

SALLY. James? Oh my God!

JAMES. The front door was open.

SALLY. Is that really you? Are you back?

JAMES. For the day.

SALLY. Look at you, you look, well, I'm not even sure what to say, you look — older. Rougher. But what are you doing here?

JAMES. *(Moving towards the wedding gown.)* It's this afternoon, isn't it?

SALLY. Why yes, yes it is. *(As James is about to touch the gown.)* French silk — please don't touch that.

JAMES. You sent me all of those sweet letters, at least once a month, with all of those charming tidbits, about the town and the school ...

SALLY. Did I tell you about my mother's new car?

JAMES. The Buick.

SALLY. And my Dad's business?

JAMES. Just booming.

SALLY. Although I am so worried about things in Europe ...

JAMES. I remember — "P.S. It's sad about Poland."

SALLY. Isn't it?

JAMES. But somehow you never mentioned Henry Lee.

SALLY. Well, he wasn't invaded, now was he?

JAMES. Oh really?

SALLY. Now James, I'm sorry, and it's not that it isn't a wonderful surprise to see you, but my parents are at the church, making sure that everything is just perfect, and my maid of honor will be here any minute. Do you remember Emmeline Atwood?

JAMES. The blind girl?

SALLY. But I told her — no dog.

JAMES. So we're alone.

SALLY. James?

JAMES. How could you? With Henry Lee?

SALLY. How could I resist? I mean, he is so handsome, and I don't want to brag, but you should have seen us, we were king and queen at the prom. Oh I'm sorry, where you were, did they even have a prom?

JAMES. Of course. And we each picked a younger, smaller boy and pretended he was our date.

SALLY. That is so sweet. Was there a theme?

JAMES. "Just Relax."

SALLY. Now James, I know that I was naughty, not to tell you about our plans. And I'm sorry that I can't invite you to the wedding, but it's a Christian ceremony, and you're, well ...

JAMES. Satan?

SALLY. *(Sincerely.)* Thank you.

JAMES. Do you love him?

SALLY. He's the President of our class ...

JAMES. Do you love him?

SALLY. My parents worship the ground he walks on ...

JAMES. Do you love him?

SALLY. Stop asking that!

JAMES. Look at me.

SALLY. I don't want to. You look crude, and unshaven, and — unreformed.

JAMES. Ever since we were little, I've known all about you. You are so good and so pretty and so perfect ...

SALLY. Because I make an effort. And I stay out of the sun.

JAMES. And today you're getting married, to the perfect boy.

SALLY. Yesireebob.

JAMES. Because you have so much in common.

SALLY. Just about everything.

JAMES. Because in just a few short hours, on your wedding night, you will both be thinking about *me*.

SALLY. You are disgusting! You are just what everyone says you are!

JAMES. A thief?

SALLY. Can you deny it?

JAMES. And a pansy?

SALLY. Well, isn't it true? Isn't that why you want Henry Lee?

JAMES. Not right now.

SALLY. James?

JAMES. I want everything. Everything beautiful.

SALLY. James?

JAMES. I want you.

SALLY. I am getting married! This afternoon!

JAMES. So there's still time.

SALLY. You went away. You left me here. So I started to hate you. So I decided to steal something. Something you wanted.

JAMES. What if I came over there, right now, and kissed you? What would you do? Would you slap my face?

SALLY. Yes I would. (*James goes to her and kisses her. She slaps him.*)

JAMES. What if I kissed you again? Would you call the police?

SALLY. Watch me. (*James kisses her again. In a tiny voice:*) Police ...

JAMES. And what if I picked you up and carried you to that bed? What if I made love to you? Would you yell stop, oh please, stop?

SALLY. Yes.

JAMES. Then goodbye. I won't make you do anything you don't want to do. (*James starts to leave.*)

SALLY. James?

JAMES. Yeah?

SALLY. Stop. *(Sally drops her robe and stands in just her slip. James picks her up, and carries her offstage, as Ludwig runs on, with a pistol.)*

LUDWIG. I am in crisis. My father is gravely ill, yet my mother is not. I can't find a bride, and I'm not ready to become king. I have been composing a note, to be discovered after my death: *(He takes out the note.)* "To my beloved parents, my brother and the nation, Do not blame yourselves. Although, of course, no one has ever truly understood or appreciated my despair. I'm sure you were all very busy. I have reached a dark crossroads, between aching futility and infinite oblivion." *(Impressed with his own words.)* This should be published. No! I am a ridiculous figure. Bavaria deserves better. Everyone deserves better. I am twenty-one years old, and there is only one solution. *(Ludwig puts the gun to his head, and as he is about to pull the trigger, we hear a gunshot, from offstage, but close by.)* What was that? *(Princess Sophie staggers onstage. She wears a period ballgown, and is played by the same actress who plays Sally. She is holding a pistol and while in great distress, is unharmed. She has a very large and pronounced humpback. Sophie is not your average princess; she's fiercely smart, and blazingly honest. She has an outcast's wit and defensiveness, but she's also just as great a romantic as Ludwig. At the moment she's tremendously upset, in agony.)*

SOPHIE. Am I bleeding? Am I dead?

LUDWIG. Who are you?

SOPHIE. I'm Princess Sophie, of Austria.

LUDWIG. But what are you doing out here, in the forest?

SOPHIE. I was out — hunting.

LUDWIG. For what?

SOPHIE. For — me!

LUDWIG. But are you all right? Are you hurt?

SOPHIE. My parents dragged me here, to the imperial ball, to be presented to that horrible Prince Ludwig. And I've never even seen a picture of him, have you? Is he so good looking?

LUDWIG. No. He has nice hair.

SOPHIE. What am I doing here? He's turned down hundreds of women. He would hate me. He would humiliate me.

LUDWIG. But why?

SOPHIE. *(Ferociously.)* Why? Why? Oh gee, I can't imagine. Let's think about that one. That's a puzzler. Why would Prince Ludwig, the Beast of Bavaria, hate a girl like me? Hmmm ... *(She uses the pistol to scratch her hump.)* could it be, it's just a wild guess, and I'm

35

really going way out on a limb here ...

LUDWIG. What?

SOPHIE. I have a HUMPBACK?

LUDWIG. You ... do?

SOPHIE. *(Turning her back to Ludwig, so he's facing her hump.)* Go ahead, touch it.

LUDWIG. No, thank you.

SOPHIE. You know you want to, everyone secretly does. Some people even think it's lucky.

LUDWIG. They do?

SOPHIE. *(Wiggling her hump, seductively.)* You could get your fondest wish.

LUDWIG. Really?

SOPHIE. I dare you. *(Ludwig touches Sophie's hump, very lightly. She screams in agony, and falls to the ground.)* OWWW!

LUDWIG. Oh my God!

SOPHIE. *(Standing up, amused.)* Kidding.

LUDWIG. What?

SOPHIE. Humpback humor.

LUDWIG. Jesus.

SOPHIE. Who are you?

LUDWIG. I'm a soldier.

SOPHIE. What's your rank?

LUDWIG. I'm — a fancy one.

SOPHIE. What are you doing here?

LUDWIG. I was out guarding the trees.

SOPHIE. Do you work for that Ludwig?

LUDWIG. Sometimes.

SOPHIE. Is it true? Is he a nightmare?

LUDWIG. No, I think he's just — a very solitary man.

SOPHIE. Oh please.

LUDWIG. He's not mean, he's just — well, he's never been allowed to make any real friends.

SOPHIE. He's a snob.

LUDWIG. No, I don't think he means to be. I think that he just spends all of his time — dreaming.

SOPHIE. Is he, you know — feeble?

LUDWIG. That's the mother.

SOPHIE. Well, I hate him. I despise him.

LUDWIG. *(Studying her, trying to be helpful.)* Have you ever thought about ... a really big corsage?

SOPHIE. No. Wait — do you have a carriage?

LUDWIG. Why?

SOPHIE. Could you take me to the railway station? Maybe I could get back to Vienna, just in time.

LUDWIG. For what?

SOPHIE. You'll think it's insane.

LUDWIG. What?

SOPHIE. But it's all I have left to live for, I've seen it twenty-eight times, but there's only one performance left.

LUDWIG. Of what?

SOPHIE. *Lohengrin.*

LUDWIG. The incredible, perfect opera?

SOPHIE. By the genius, Richard Wagner? Do you know it?

LUDWIG. Only every note!

SOPHIE. Stop it! *(They both scream, with surprise and delight.)*

LUDWIG and SOPHIE. AHHH!

LUDWIG. Elsa, the innocent maiden ...

SOPHIE. And her brother, who's bewitched into a swan ...

LUDWIG. And then Elsa's accused of his murder ...

SOPHIE. Until they're both saved by a handsome young knight! When did you see it?

LUDWIG. Only once.

SOPHIE. Why?

LUDWIG. It was two years ago, in Berlin. I was — on leave. But I'd been dreaming about it for months, I couldn't think about anything else. But then, during the performance, it was all too beautiful, and I was — overcome. I started sobbing uncontrollably, and my body wouldn't stop shaking.

SOPHIE. Sometimes I vomit.

LUDWIG. I foamed at the mouth.

SOPHIE. Sometimes I become completely incontinent.

LUDWIG. *(Impressed.)* You're good.

SOPHIE. But why didn't you go back?

LUDWIG. I was too ashamed.

SOPHIE. I know. Usually I wear a big cape, and I try to sit way in the back, but people still see me.

LUDWIG. My family worries all the time that I'll completely disgrace them.

SOPHIE. And my mother, she keeps saying that I'll never marry anyone. And just before I leave the house, she always tells me the most awful thing.

LUDWIG. What?

SOPHIE. "Stand up straight."

LUDWIG. That's unbearable.

SOPHIE. I hate my life.

LUDWIG. I hate mine.

SOPHIE. Let's kill ourselves.

LUDWIG. Right now. *(They face each other and put the barrels of their guns into each other's mouths. Garbled.)* One ...

SOPHIE. *(Garbled.)* Two ...

LUDWIG. *(Garbled.)* Sophie?

SOPHIE. *(Garbled.)* Yes?

LUDWIG. *(They remove the guns from each other's mouths.)* Sophie, I know this is very sudden, but you're the only person I've ever met who doesn't think I'm strange.

SOPHIE. But you are.

LUDWIG. Sophie?

SOPHIE. But that's wonderful. Because I'm even worse.

LUDWIG. How?

SOPHIE. *(Making a bell-ringing Quasimodo gesture.)* Ding-dong.

LUDWIG. But when I look at you, I don't see something strange. I see someone who's — enchanted.

SOPHIE. How?

LUDWIG. You know how in the stories, sometimes there's a magical dwarf or a sly troll?

SOPHIE. Where are you going with this?

LUDWIG. But that doesn't make them ugly. Maybe your hump is a sign of magic. Of true beauty.

SOPHIE. It is?

LUDWIG. You're a princess. You belong in a castle.

SOPHIE. Don't you just love castles?

LUDWIG. More than anything. More than breathing. More than my own life. I love castles more than — chocolate. *(He gasps.)* I can't believe I said that!

SOPHIE. Everyone is happy in a castle.

LUDWIG. But not those modern castles, which are really just big houses, but a storybook castle.

SOPHIE. All the way up on a mountaintop, with banners and turrets ...

LUDWIG. Floating above the clouds ...

SOPHIE. The home of the gods ...

LUDWIG. The most beautiful place on earth ...

LUDWIG and SOPHIE. Valhalla.

LUDWIG. Marry me?

SOPHIE. Yes.

LUDWIG. Oh my God.

SOPHIE. But wait — I don't even know your name. *(Pfeiffer enters.)*

PFEIFFER. Your Highness?

SOPHIE. *(Taken aback.)* Your Highness?

PFEIFFER. *(To Sophie.)* Prince Ludwig.

SOPHIE. Prince Ludwig? *(Sophie, realizing who Ludwig really is, falls into a curtsy, although she's furious.)*

LUDWIG. The liar.

SOPHIE. Oh no. Oh my God. You are a beast, how could you do this, were you on a scavenger hunt, find one peacock feather and a humpback?

LUDWIG. No. I would never do anything to hurt you, please Sophie, you have to believe me. Because that was the most perfect conversation I've ever had. And I meant every word.

SOPHIE. You did?

PFEIFFER. I'm sorry, I'm confused. But Your Highness, you must come with me at once. It's your father, I'm afraid he's taken a turn.

LUDWIG. Maybe — I can cheer him.

PFEIFFER. How?

LUDWIG. Pfeiffer, I think, I hope — that I'm engaged.

PFEIFFER. You are?

SOPHIE. *(After a beat.)* Yes, we are.

PFEIFFER. *(Very pleased.)* Well, congratulations.

SOPHIE. Thank you.

PFEIFFER. Have you met?

LUDWIG. Yes. At last.

PFEIFFER. I knew that you could do it. You are becoming such a fine young man.

LUDWIG. I am?

SOPHIE. Yes you are.

LUDWIG. *(To Sophie.)* I'm sorry, I have to go.

PFEIFFER. But first — a kiss?

LUDWIG. *(Taken aback.)* Pfeiffer!

SOPHIE. He means me. We could kiss, like in *Lohengrin.* As if we were in a castle.

PFEIFFER. A castle?

LUDWIG. My Elsa.

SOPHIE. My hero.

PFEIFFER. My prayers. *(Ludwig and Sophie hand their pistols to Pfeiffer, and then they move towards each other, theatrically, like operatic lovers. Ludwig lifts Sophie off the ground. They kiss, as sweepingly romantic music is heard. Ludwig lowers Sophie and they move apart, gracefully.)*

LUDWIG. I have kissed.

SOPHIE. I am saved.

PFEIFFER. Your Highness?

LUDWIG. Adieu! *(Ludwig leaves, on a cloud of joy.)*

SOPHIE. Do I look different? Don't answer that.

PFEIFFER. You look — beautiful.

SOPHIE. He is so special.

PFEIFFER. You have no idea.

SOPHIE. What an incredible day. Just this morning, I was the loneliest humpback in Europe.

PFEIFFER. Was there a contest?

SOPHIE. And then I came out here, to kill myself, and then I meet — my Prince. And suddenly the moonlight is so warm. Do you know what that sounds like?

PFEIFFER. A fairy tale?

SOPHIE. A happy ending. *(As Sophie exits, elated, the Queen enters, from the opposite side of the stage. She is deeply mournful, and dressed entirely in black.)*

QUEEN. There is tragic news. My husband, the king, is dead.

PFEIFFER. But your son is engaged.

QUEEN. *(Instantly ecstatic, pumping her fists in the air.)* Yes!

PFEIFFER. Your Highness?

QUEEN. Wait — is he engaged to a very beautiful girl? One who will break his heart, and destroy the monarchy? A Lola Montes?

PFEIFFER. She's a humpback.

QUEEN. *(Even more ecstatic, to heaven.)* Thank you! *(As the Queen runs off, Pfeiffer turns to the audience.)*

PFEIFFER. Nobles, citizens, peasants — in the back. We live in extraordinary times. It is with great joy that I introduce your brand new monarch, a regent of only the brightest promise. Please welcome — King Ludwig Freidrich Wilhelm II of Bavaria! *(Grand processional music is heard, along with a roaring crowd. Ludwig enters, as a spotlight hits him. He is now dressed in the full, sumptuous royal regalia of the Order of the Knights of St. George. He is resplendent, in a mountainous cape of heavily gold embroidered blue velvet, trimmed with yards of ermine. He wears a crown, a lace jabot, gauntleted gloves and white satin leggings and shoes. His wardrobe is based on the glo-rious royal portrait painted by George Schachinger in 1887. Ludwig is radiant, tearful and ecstatic, clutching his golden scepter — he's like someone who's just won an Academy Award. He faces the audience.)*

LUDWIG. I can't believe this! Thank you, thank you all so much … um, while I am not accustomed to public speaking … *(He takes a scrap of paper from his sleeve and glances at it — his acceptance speech.)* I would just like to say that — I am very proud to be your new king. *(The Queen stands beside Ludwig, hissing directions at him.)*

QUEEN. Shoulders back! And what are you wearing?

LUDWIG. It's a coronation!

QUEEN. *(Regarding Ludwig's outfit.)* That's a couch!

LUDWIG. *(To the crowd.)* First of all, I would like to thank my father, for dying …

QUEEN. And who else?

LUDWIG. And I would also like to thank my mother, the griev-ing royal widow …

QUEEN. *(Gesturing, to her all-black outfit.)* It's slimming.

LUDWIG. *(To the crowd.)* And I promise that I will try my very best to be — a good king.

QUEEN. We can't hear you!

LUDWIG. A GOOD KING!

QUEEN. *(To the crowd, grabbing Ludwig's chin, affectionately.)* Is that a face?

LUDWIG. And I'd just like to add that — I adore Bavaria!

QUEEN. Butch it up, Betty!

LUDWIG. *(To the Queen.)* Shut the hell up! *(Another ovation is heard, in response to Ludwig's last remark. The Queen, delighted by Ludwig's newfound strength and command, mimes zipping her lip. Emboldened.)* I would like our nation to become — a beacon of beauty. And so for my very first official act, I am going to the opera, to see Lohengrin! *(Ludwig sits on an impressive golden chair or stool, and watches the Dainsville wedding as if he were at the opera, watching Lohengrin. He speaks the words of a letter he will write to Sophie. The Queen sits beside him. Enraptured:)* My dearest Sophie, as the curtain rose, I felt a thunderclap of purest happiness.

QUEEN. *(Speaking to heaven.)* My dearest husband, you would be so proud of our son.

LUDWIG. The orchestra, the lights, and then — we approach the close of the act, as the townspeople gather at the glorious cathedral of Brabant. *(Reverend Howesberry enters; he's a fire-and-brimstone*

41

Texas preacher. He will be played by the same actor who plays Pfeiffer.)
REVEREND. Welcome, one and all, to the All Souls First Baptist Church, of Dainsville, Texas! I'm Reverend Howesberry, and we're gonna have us a wedding!
LUDWIG. Lohengrin enters, in gleaming armor!
REVEREND. I like a man in uniform!
QUEEN. *(To Ludwig.)* I like you in that crown. *(Henry Lee, in an army uniform, enters and approaches the altar.)*
HENRY LEE. *(Speaking his thoughts.)* I'm going to get married ...
LUDWIG. He's going to be married ...
REVEREND. He's gonna get married!
QUEEN. *(To heaven, regarding Ludwig.)* Our boy is getting married!
HENRY LEE. To Sally ...
LUDWIG. To Elsa ...
QUEEN. *(Thrilled.)* To a humpback!
EVERYONE. Here we go! *(We hear the "Wedding March," from* Lohengrin *as Sally enters the church in a wedding gown, with her veil covering her face. She approaches the altar.)*
LUDWIG. As the bride approached the altar, a perfect melody rang forth, stately yet passionate, yearning yet proud. It is called the "Wedding March."
QUEEN. The "Wedding March"!
HENRY LEE. The "Wedding March" ...
REVEREND. It's a catchy tune!
QUEEN. *(To Ludwig.)* It's our song!
LUDWIG. As the music soared, I entered what I can only call an escalating trance. Note upon note, pleasure upon pleasure ...
REVEREND. Do you, Henry Lee Stafford, take this woman, Sally Ann Mortimer, to be your lawfully wedded wife? *(As Henry Lee opens his mouth to reply, he begins lip-synching to a glorious tenor aria, from Wagner.)*
LUDWIG. He is strong, he is stalwart ...
QUEEN. *(To heaven, regarding Ludwig.)* He is strong, he is stalwart ...
HENRY LEE. *(To himself.)* I am strong, I am stalwart ...
QUEEN. *(To heaven, regarding Ludwig.)* He is going to be a husband!
HENRY LEE. *(To himself.)* I am going to be a husband ...
REVEREND. *(To Henry Lee.)* You're gonna be a husband!
LUDWIG. *(Staring at Sally.)* And look at her tiny little shoes! I'm dying!

QUEEN.	REVEREND.	HENRY LEE.
(To Ludwig.)	*(To Henry Lee.)*	*(To himself.)*
Be a man!	Be a man!	Be a man!

REVEREND. And do you, Sally Ann Mortimer, take this man, Henry Lee Stafford, to be your lawfully wedded husband? *(As Sally opens her mouth to reply, she lip-synchs to a glorious soprano aria.)* Ain't she purty?

LUDWIG. She's so lovely!

HENRY LEE. She's my wife ...

QUEEN. *(To Ludwig.)* Girls are good.

LUDWIG. I am there!

QUEEN. We are there!

REVEREND. We're almost there!

HENRY LEE. I need some air ...

LUDWIG. I am music!

REVEREND. I am ready!

QUEEN. I am complete!

HENRY LEE. I am not beautiful!

LUDWIG. I am in a state of ecstasy ...

QUEEN. I am in a state of bliss ...

HENRY LEE. I am in a state of panic ...

REVEREND. By the authority vested in me, by the glorious state of Texas ... *(The Reverend begins to lip-synch to something grandly operatic.)*

SALLY. Not so fast! *(Sally has entered, from offstage or the back of the house. She is disheveled, wearing only her slip.)*

HENRY LEE. *(Stunned.)* Sally?

REVEREND. *(Stunned.)* Sally Mortimer?

QUEEN. *(To Ludwig.)* Who is that?

LUDWIG. *(Following the action.)* Ortrud has entered! A jealous pagan princess! She seeks to sabotage the nuptials!

SALLY. He tied me up! Then he stole my gown, and my daddy's Cadillac!

QUEEN. She seems upset.

HENRY LEE. Who did?

SALLY. The bride!

REVEREND. The *bride?* *(A police siren begins to wail.)*

HENRY LEE. The bride?

LUDWIG. *(Thrilled.)* The French horns! *(The bride lifts her veil, so we can see her face — it's James, wearing Sally's wedding gown.)*

SALLY, HENRY LEE and REVEREND. *(Realizing it's James.)* James!

JAMES. I think I'm gonna cry.

QUEEN. I think I'm gonna burst!

HENRY LEE. I think I'm gonna die!

LUDWIG. I think I'm gonna faint!

SALLY. *(To James.)* I think I'm gonna kill you!

REVEREND. *(To Sally.)* I think I'm gonna help you! *(The Reverend takes out a sawed-off shotgun, which he passes to Henry Lee, who hands it to Sally.)*

SALLY. *(To James.)* I think you'd better run.

LUDWIG. It is all too beautiful!

JAMES. Sally ...

SALLY. *(Aiming the gun at James.)* One ...

LUDWIG. I am home!

JAMES. Henry Lee ...

HENRY LEE. Two ...

QUEEN. You're the king!

JAMES. I think I'm gonna go. *(James, running out, tosses his bouquet to Ludwig, who catches it.)*

REVEREND. God help us all!

SALLY, HENRY LEE and REVEREND. Three! *(Sally fires the shotgun across the stage at James, as he exits. Ludwig faints, dead away, to the floor. The Queen looks at him, then at the audience. She realizes that everyone is staring at her, and her unconscious son. She smiles graciously.)*

QUEEN. Intermission. *(Curtain.)*

ACT TWO

*A pinspot appears on Ludwig's face. He is enraptured, trans-
ported, perhaps with his eyes shut, and his mouth hanging
open in bliss. He is listening to something from* Tannhauser
and he is utterly transfixed by the music. He drools.

PFEIFFER. *(From the darkness.)* Your Highness! *(No response; the
music continues.)* Your Highness! *(The lights come up on the throne room,
in Munich. This will be suggested mostly by having Ludwig sprawled on
the ornate, golden imperial throne. Maps, books and documents are piled
nearby. Ludwig wears his crown and a daytime uniform, which is still
fairly gaudy. Pfeiffer stands close by, holding a sheaf of documents. The*
Tannhauser *music ends abruptly.)*

LUDWIG. *(Gradually returning to reality.)* Yes?

PFEIFFER. You were doing it again. You were gone.

LUDWIG. I was in *Tannhauser.* I was a handsome young knight,
lured into an enchanted, sensuous grotto. And I was surrounded by
satyrs and satin and orgies.

PFEIFFER. Have you even glanced at the treaty proposal?

LUDWIG. Pfeiffer, what's an orgy?

PFEIFFER. It's when vicious, depraved philistines have sex in a
group.

LUDWIG. Is it heavenly?

PFEIFFER. Yes.

LUDWIG. Then let's have one — by royal decree!

PFEIFFER. Your Highness, shall I call in a guard to paddle your
buttocks?

LUDWIG. Really?

PFEIFFER. If you focus.

LUDWIG. *(Tossing a pile of documents into the air.)* But I'm in agony!

PFEIFFER. *(As he begins to pick up the documents, from the floor.)*
You're in Munich. And you've only been king for a year. And you've
been doing so well.

LUDWIG. I have?

PFEIFFER. But this month alone you've already been to the opera

eighteen times. Three *Tannhausers*, five *Tristans*, two *Meistersingers* ...
LUDWIG. And eight *Lohengrins*!
PFEIFFER. It's like a drug!
LUDWIG. Do you know the true tragedy of Lohengrin?
PFEIFFER. What?
LUDWIG. That he could never go to see *Lohengrin*.
PFEIFFER. *(Exasperated.)* Your Highness!
LUDWIG. I know. You're right. And that's why I'm chaining myself to this throne.
PFEIFFER. You're what?
LUDWIG. *(Ludwig begins to handcuff himself to his throne, with cuffs or manacles.)* I want to be a good king. So no more opera, I'm giving it up.
PFEIFFER. Are you sure about this?
LUDWIG. Yes. And here's the key. *(He hands Pfeiffer the key.)* And I forbid you to unlock me, no matter how much I beg, under no circumstances, absolutely no opera.
PFEIFFER. Truly?
LUDWIG. I can beat this.
PFEIFFER. Very good. Because we may very well be going to war.
LUDWIG. With whom?
PFEIFFER. With Prussia.
LUDWIG. Excellent. Now explain the situation. And this time, I promise, I will pay complete attention and follow every word.
PFEIFFER. All right. It's a border dispute. Bismarck, the Prussian Chancellor, has taken control of the Duchy of Schleswig, while Emperor Franz Josef of Austria rules the neighboring Holstein.
LUDWIG. Schleswig-Holstein.
PFEIFFER. Correct. Now, Bismarck wants to build a canal on the Baltic, across Holstein to the North Sea, while Franz Josef demands that Prussia return several provinces annexed a hundred years ago by Freidrich the Great.
LUDWIG. Aha!
PFEIFFER. But Bismarck has been feuding with Denmark, while Franz Josef has engaged in preliminary sessions with the Duke of Augustenburg, a pretender to the Duchies. And here's where it gets really fascinating ...
LUDWIG. Pfeiffer?
PFEIFFER. Yes?
LUDWIG. Pfeiffer, I need it.
PFEIFFER. What?

LUDWIG. Just a few notes. An aria. A first act.

PFEIFFER. No!

LUDWIG. But the opera house is only a few blocks away, the curtain's in just twenty minutes, I have to go or I'll die, please unlock me.

PFEIFFER. I said *no*.

LUDWIG. Good. Thank you. I was testing you.

PFEIFFER. I thought so.

LUDWIG. *(Sagely.)* Oo-hoo.

PFEIFFER. *(Agreeing.)* Oo-hoo.

LUDWIG. Instead, I'd like to commission a reliquary. From Faberge, the goldsmith to the Tsars.

PFEIFFER. A reliquary?

LUDWIG. I want hammered gold, worked with precious gems. After my death, it will contain my heart.

PFEIFFER. Your heart?

LUDWIG. Shattered! From paperwork!

PFEIFFER. Your Highness!

LUDWIG. Please, Pfeiffer, I'm begging you, I'll give you anything you want, what would you like — a title? An estate? Belgium?

PFEIFFER. No!

LUDWIG. I'm the king, I'm commanding you! You have to unlock me! If I don't see an opera, I don't know what will happen. I'll collapse, I'll explode, I'll start — going to the ballet. Is that what you want?

PFEIFFER. No!

LUDWIG. Or I'll chew off my arm! I'll do it, Pfeiffer, you know I will, I'm starting, I'm gnawing at my flesh, watch me, you'll be held responsible for the cannibal king ... *(As he chews on his arm savagely.)* It's tasty ...

PFEIFFER. Why? So you can go see some ridiculous story, like that one about dragons and mermaids?

LUDWIG. *The Ring!*

PFEIFFER. And who was that woman, on horseback?

LUDWIG. Brunhilde?

PFEIFFER. Yes.

LUDWIG. She's a warrior goddess. And yes, I know, you're right, it's ridiculous, that soprano was so — hefty.

PFEIFFER. With those big meaty arms.

LUDWIG. And those legs, like tree trunks.

PFEIFFER. *(Turned on.)* I liked her.

LUDWIG. Pfeiffer?

PFEIFFER. I have always had an affinity for — robust women. My mother was unthinkably beautiful, at nearly 400 pounds. My birth wasn't discovered for three days. And there was my one true love, Calpurnia, at college. She was six-foot-four, all mammoth muscle, but then I lost her forever — even now, how I hate the circus.

LUDWIG. Of course.

PFEIFFER. But then, at the performance the other evening, I was yawning, dozing, wondering will it ever end, and suddenly ...

LUDWIG and PFEIFFER. Brunhilde!

PFEIFFER. And every midnight since, as I try to sleep, I tell myself, no, Pfeiffer, it was an illusion, no, Pfeiffer, it was the costume — armor can be cruelly deceptive ...

LUDWIG. Honey ...

PFEIFFER. I must not allow myself to imagine, to hallucinate, to dream that she is singing only to me, my tiny head wedged like a trembling walnut between the iron cannons of her Himalayan thighs, no, they are not merely thighs ...

LUDWIG. Oh no!

PFEIFFER. They are twin teutonic armies, pounding, squeezing, drowning me ecstatically in endless amazon acres of pure, pink, powerful woman flesh ...

LUDWIG. Time for the opera?

PFEIFFER. Let's go! *(Pfeiffer, on fire with lust, runs out.)*

LUDWIG. The key! Pfeiffer, hold the curtain! *(Ludwig, struggling helplessly, still chained, begins to drag the throne offstage with him, pursuing Pfeiffer. Lights down on Munich. We hear the sound of a ship's bell. Lights up on the deck of an army transport ship, somewhere in the middle of the Atlantic. This is indicated by ocean sounds and a fragment of railing. Henry Lee enters, in an army uniform and overcoat. He looks out to sea. He lights a cigarette. James enters, also wearing an army uniform and overcoat.)*

JAMES. Hey there. *(Henry Lee stares at him.)*

HENRY LEE. No. No.

JAMES. Hey there, soldier.

HENRY LEE. *What the fuck are you doing on this ship?*

JAMES. Okay, I know that you're really mad at me and that you hate me and you wish I was dead, so I should just tell you something. Right after I had sex with Sally, and put on her gown, and came to the church, I felt really terrible.

HENRY LEE. Why?

JAMES. The sleeves.

HENRY LEE. Fuck you! *(Just as Henry Lee is about to throw James over the railing, a uniformed sergeant appears. He is very stern and macho, and he's played by the same actor who plays Pfeiffer.)*

SERGEANT. Soldiers! *(James and Henry Lee snap to attention, saluting.)* Ten-hut!

JAMES and HENRY LEE. Sir, yes, sir!

SERGEANT. What are you two doing out here?

HENRY LEE. Keeping watch, sir!

SERGEANT. And is that all?

HENRY LEE. Yes, sir!

JAMES. He was touching me, sir!

SERGEANT. *(To Henry Lee.)* Private, is that true? Are you some kind of butt-toucher? Some kind of pecker-puffer?

HENRY LEE. No, sir!

SERGEANT. But why not?

HENRY LEE. Sir?

SERGEANT. *(To Henry Lee, regarding James.)* He's adorable! Get busy! As you were.

JAMES and HENRY LEE. *(Saluting.)* Sir, yes, sir! *(The sergeant exits.)*

HENRY LEE. What was that?

JAMES. A friend.

HENRY LEE. James, I am warning you. Despite your very best efforts, Sally and I got married, right on schedule. So I do not want to see your psychotic little pinhead, I do not want to hear your perverted little chitchat, I do not want to know that you are within one million miles! Go below!

JAMES. I want to smoke.

HENRY LEE. So do I!

JAMES. Fine.

HENRY LEE. Fine! So you just stay way the hell over there!

JAMES. And you just stay way, way the hell over there.

HENRY LEE. Fine!

JAMES. Fine. *(Henry Lee stands on one side of the stage, James all the way over on the other. They both smoke. Henry Lee is turned away from James, vigorously ignoring him. James watches Henry Lee. He begins whistling a little tune.)*

HENRY LEE. *(Cutting James off, holding out a hand, still not looking at him, still furious.)* Eh!

JAMES. Henry Lee …

HENRY LEE. *(Cutting him off, still not looking at him.)* No!

JAMES. Don't you just hate Hitler?

HENRY LEE. Shut up!

JAMES. Henry Lee, I know you. And I know that you are secretly thrilled beyond all measure to see me. Because you need me more than ever.

HENRY LEE. Do you know what terrifies me?

JAMES. Everything?

HENRY LEE. No. What terrifies me is that sometimes, I listen to you. And I realize that you actually believe what you're saying.

JAMES. Because I'm right. Because we have finally done it, just like I promised. We have left Texas! We're on our way!

HENRY LEE. To World War II, you moron! Have you seen the guys on this ship? After lights out, half of 'em start crying.

JAMES. I hear 'em.

HENRY LEE. I'm scared shitless. Why aren't you?

JAMES. If you don't want to die, you just have to be in the right movie.

HENRY LEE. We are not in a movie!

JAMES. Why not? If we're in a war movie, sure, we could get killed, by a tank or a torpedo or a character actor.

HENRY LEE. A character actor?

JAMES. But if we're in, say, a screwball comedy or a musical, everything's deco and beautiful and nobody ever dies.

HENRY LEE. But we're not! We're on a rusty tin crate, like sitting ducks.

JAMES. Like in *Anchors Aweigh* or *Follow the Fleet* or *Soldiers and Seamen*.

HENRY LEE. *Soldiers and Seamen?*

JAMES. That's our movie. And if we sing the title song, we'll be perfectly safe. All of the German U-boats will hear us and say … *(In a German accent.)* "Hold your fire! Vait until ze ballad!"

HENRY LEE. Goodbye. *(As Henry Lee is about to exit:)*

JAMES. *(Starting to sing, improvising.)*
AHOY THERE, MATEY
AND SET THOSE SAILS
WE'RE A TRANSPORT SHIP
FILLED WITH U.S. MALES
WE'RE SINGING AND DANCING
WE'RE A TALENTED BOAT
BECAUSE SOLDIERS NEED SEAMEN
TO KEEP THEM AFLOAT

HENRY LEE. What are you?

JAMES.
>   AVAST ME HEARTIES, WE'RE BUILT TO LAST
>   MY POOPDECK'S FILLED
>   WITH YOUR MIZZENMAST
>   YOUR PORTHOLE'S EMPTY
>   AND YOU'VE GOT TO LEARN
>   THAT SOLDIERS NEED SEAMEN
>   FROM STEM TO STERN

HENRY LEE. You should be court-martialed!

JAMES. This is the dancing part. *(As he dances around Henry Lee:)* Work with me.

HENRY LEE. Never.

JAMES. You know you want to.

HENRY LEE. I do not!

JAMES. You're itchin' to. Every cell in your body is cryin' out.

HENRY LEE. I do not sing. I do not dance. I'm married.

JAMES. *(Singing.)*
>   THE ARMY, THE NAVY
>   WHO SHOULD BE IN CHARGE?
>   WHILE SEAMEN ARE HE-MEN ...

HENRY LEE. *(Struggling not to say it, resisting every second, angrily.)*
>   OUR PRIVATES ARE LARGE.

JAMES. Henry Lee.

HENRY LEE. What?

JAMES. That was great.

HENRY LEE. I don't care. I shouldn't have said it. I didn't. That wasn't me.

JAMES.
>   SOLDIERS WEAR CUTE COMBAT BOOTS
>   SEAMEN SALUTE THOSE RECRUITS
>   AN UNORTHODOX HOLE ...

HENRY LEE.
>   IS FOUND IN A FOXHOLE

JAMES.
>   THE FLEET'S IN, BUT WHO'S IN THE FLEET?
>   WE'LL BE ETHEL MERMANS

HENRY LEE.
>   AND CRUSH ALL THOSE GERMANS

JAMES and HENRY LEE.
>   BY SINGING THEM INTO DEFEAT!

(They do a little shave-and-a-haircut dance move together. Henry Lee

stares at his feet, shocked at what they've just done.)

JAMES. *(Proudly, to an unseen crowd.)* My husband!

HENRY LEE. *(Furious.)* James! *(Henry Lee strides offstage.)*

JAMES. *(Following him.)* Sweetheart? *(James follows Henry Lee offstage. Lights down on the ship, as Ludwig enters, on horseback. His horse might be a wire and papier-maché contraption which he wears around his waist. Ludwig wears a parade dress uniform, including a cape and a plumed hat. Both Ludwig and his steed are attired in white and gold. Ludwig's horse is led by Pfeiffer. As Ludwig reviews the troops, he and Pfeiffer look into the audience.)*

PFEIFFER. The Twenty-third Regiment, Your Highness. *(Ludwig nods and salutes.)* The Twenty-fourth Regiment, Your Highness. *(Ludwig nods and salutes.)* The Twenty-fifth Regiment, Your Highness.

LUDWIG. Excuse me, how many regiments in all?

PFEIFFER. Five hundred and twelve, Your Highness.

LUDWIG. *(In despair.)* My *wrist.*

PFEIFFER. These young men are about to go into battle against Prussia. Most of them have never been away from home. You can give them hope.

LUDWIG. But how?

PFEIFFER. You're their king, their champion, their — Lohengrin.

LUDWIG. I am?

PFEIFFER. And Prussia resembles — who's the villain, in the opera?

LUDWIG. The brutal Count Telramund, who tries to get rid of Elsa and steal her land. So she prays for a miracle.

PFEIFFER. And then you appear!

LUDWIG. *(Emboldened, to the troops.)* Gentlemen — you are all so brave and so noble and some of you are so attractive …

PFEIFFER. Your Highness!

LUDWIG. Whenever I seek courage, there is only one source. Many years ago, on a battlefield much like this, a lovely maiden appeared … *(Sophie runs on, dressed as a medieval maiden, in a flowing velvet gown, with a long braided blonde wig. Enchanted music is heard.)*

SOPHIE. My knight! My savior!

LUDWIG. Elsa!

SOPHIE. You must save me from the brutal Count Telramund!

LUDWIG. Summon the scoundrel! *(The Queen enters, dressed as the evil Count, in dashing black and gold; she is hooded, so only her eyes and mouth are visible. She is also on mechanical horseback — a black stallion. Darker, more villainous music.)*

QUEEN. Greetings, vagabond!

LUDWIG. Hail, knave!

QUEEN. They say that you dare to challenge my evil.

LUDWIG. I dare!

QUEEN. They say that you champion the pure and the powerless.

LUDWIG. I shall!

QUEEN. And they claim that you possess inhuman, supernatural powers.

SOPHIE. It's true!

LUDWIG. I'm a tenor!

QUEEN. En garde, knight of goodness!

LUDWIG. Taste my steel, hound of hell! *(Ludwig and the Queen howl war cries and ride at each other, jousting with their swords or lances, to appropriately rousing music. They both miss.)*

PFEIFFER. Miss!

QUEEN. Coward! Stripling!

LUDWIG. Your evil is strong.

QUEEN. Your virtue is pale.

LUDWIG. Your steed is sturdy.

QUEEN. Your stallion is small.

LUDWIG. *(To his horse.)* Don't listen!

PFEIFFER. Ride! *(Ludwig and the Queen repeat their war cries and ride at one another. Just as they are about to joust:)*

SOPHIE. I love you, my hero!

LUDWIG. *(Distracted.)* What?

PFEIFFER. Miss! *(The knights have again missed each other entirely.)*

SOPHIE. I'm sorry! I got carried away!

LUDWIG. *(Regarding Sophie.)* She's a virgin.

SOPHIE. But I don't want to be!

QUEEN. So why haven't you married him? You've been engaged for over two years.

LUDWIG. Hold on — this part isn't in the opera.

SOPHIE. I'm doing my best. I'm here in his fantasy.

QUEEN. I don't care. The real world is waiting. Are you squeamish?

SOPHIE. He's sensitive!

QUEEN. Are you strange?

SOPHIE. He's shy!

QUEEN. Is he a cream puff? A sacher torte? A sissy?

LUDWIG. Who are you, my mother?

QUEEN. *(Ripping off her hood.)* Yes! And I am stronger than your fantasy!

LUDWIG. *(Raising his sword.)* My fantasy will rule!

PFEIFFER. The final joust!

QUEEN. You must behave! You must surrender!

LUDWIG. I must keep dreaming! I must take flight!

QUEEN. But that is madness.

LUDWIG. That is glory!

PFEIFFER. Raise your swords!

LUDWIG. *(Raising his sword.)* For beauty!

QUEEN. For duty!

SOPHIE. *(Regarding Ludwig.)* My cutie!

PFEIFFER. Ride! *(They ride at each other, and Ludwig stabs the Queen, who is mortally wounded.)*

QUEEN. I am vanquished! He has slain me! His own mother! *(The Queen collapses on the ground, dead. The Queen moans, theatrically. She raises her head.)*

PFEIFFER. But lo, she rises!

QUEEN. A prophecy, milord. In fantasy, dreamers flourish. But in life, soldiers bleed. Kingdoms fall.

PFEIFFER. *(Clapping his hands, sharply.)* Your Highness! Your Highness!

LUDWIG. Yes? *(Sophie and the Queen exit, as Ludwig returns to reality.)*

PFEIFFER. You were speaking to the troops, you were sharing an inspirational tale, and you drifted off.

LUDWIG. *(To the troops, sincerely.)* I'm sorry! Be brave!

PFEIFFER. The Twenty-sixth Regiment, Your Highness. *(As Ludwig nods and salutes, lights down on the battlefield, as James and Henry Lee run on from the opposite side of the stage, having just parachuted into Bavaria. Their parachutes billow on the ground behind them, and they try to bunch them up.)*

JAMES. Where are we?

HENRY LEE. We should be about fifty miles from the German border, in Bavaria.

JAMES. *(Looking around, excited.)* Bavaria!

HENRY LEE. Fold your chute!

JAMES. I will, but this is so amazing! We just parachuted out of a plane, behind enemy lines, together!

HENRY LEE. We are not together! We are charting enemy troop positions, and we have to try not to get captured or killed.

JAMES. Right. And we have to stay away from the main roads.

HENRY LEE. Yes.

JAMES. And locate bunkers and ammunition depots.

HENRY LEE. Good.

JAMES. And then we eliminate that Von Trapp family.

HENRY LEE. *(Fed up, leaving.)* See you in France.

JAMES. Come back, I'll behave, I swear.

HENRY LEE. We need to radio the base, and tell them our location.

JAMES. *(Using binoculars.)* Okay, transmit these coordinates.

HENRY LEE. *(Using a walkie-talkie.)* Go.

JAMES. We are standing approximately half a kilometer from the target drop, north by northeast.

HENRY LEE. *(Staring out towards the audience.)* James?

JAMES. *(Still using the binoculars.)* There's open farmland with haystacks and a barn, we seem to have landed in an enormous placemat ...

HENRY LEE. James. *(James lowers the binoculars and sees that Henry Lee now has his hands raised over his head. James immediately takes out his pistol, and points it towards the audience.)*

JAMES. *(Threatening.)* Achtung! Halten sie! Schnell!

HENRY LEE. *(To James.)* What are you doing? He's got a gun!

JAMES. So do I. *(To the unseen Nazi.)* Throw it down, or I will kill you. I will shoot you. Bang bang!

HENRY LEE. He threw down his gun! Do it! Shoot him!

JAMES. No.

HENRY LEE. Kill him! Shoot him! He's a Nazi!

JAMES. *(To the soldier; gesturing.)* Run! Go! Now! *(James and Henry Lee watch the soldier run off.)*

HENRY LEE. Oh my God, Jesus Christ ...

JAMES. Henry Lee!

HENRY LEE. You — you saved my life.

JAMES. Yes I did!

HENRY LEE. But why — why didn't you shoot him?

JAMES. If he had made a move, if he had touched you, I would have took his head clean off, I know it. But I looked at him and — he looked back. It was amazing. I mean, he's our age. And every-thing about him told me that he didn't want to do it, that's why he hadn't shot both of us, already. He was beautiful. *(A siren begins to sound, and dogs begin to bark, as a searchlight sweeps across the stage, catching James and Henry Lee in its glare.)* Move! *(We hear the sound of machine-gun fire, and James and Henry Lee run offstage. Music rises through the gunfire. Through the music, we hear the voices of Pfeiffer, the Queen, Sophie and others, all calling out, "Ludwig!" Henry Lee's parachute sweeps across the stage, eventually covering*

Ludwig, who is lying on the stage floor, in his shirt and underwear; the rest of his clothing is heaped nearby. Princess Sophie enters.)

SOPHIE. Ludwig!

LUDWIG. Sophie?

SOPHIE. They've scheduled our wedding, for this Saturday. But first, I just have to ask — what are you doing out here, at center stage, at the Royal Court Opera House? *(A handsome young opera singer enters, from offstage. He's bare chested, or tucking in his shirt; he's just finished putting on his clothes. He's eager and genuine, if not all that bright. He will be played by the same actor who plays Henry Lee.)*

SINGER. *(To Ludwig.)* Oh, 'scuse me, I thought we were like, alone ...

SOPHIE. No, it's fine.

SINGER. *(To Ludwig.)* Last night was totally fun, like out here on the floor, but just now, when I was grabbing my stuff, I put it together — you're the king, right?

LUDWIG. Indeed.

SINGER. *(Delighted.)* I knew I recognized you — from the money.

LUDWIG. Yes.

SINGER. And whoa — you're Princess Sophie, of Austria!

SOPHIE. Two for two.

SINGER. *(Thrilled.)* My sister has a humpback — she worships you!

SOPHIE. She does?

SINGER. I mean before, she got like all bummed about it, but now, since you two got engaged, she's super-proud. She collects pictures of you, and the guys are like, all over her. And her best friend, Inga, she's got like a clubfoot, but I'm like, chh!

SOPHIE. Really?

SINGER. *(Gesturing, respectfully, to Sophie's hump.)* Could I?

SOPHIE. Sure. *(The singer delicately touches Sophie's hump.)*

SINGER. *(Beyond thrilled.)* Whoa! *(Holding up the hand that touched the hump.)* I'm gonna keep this! *(To Sophie and Ludwig.)* Later!

LUDWIG. *(The singer exits.)* Do you know who that was? Think about it.

SOPHIE. It can't be.

LUDWIG. Yet it is.

SOPHIE. Don't say it!

LUDWIG. That was Lohengrin, from last night's performance.

SOPHIE. Oh no!

LUDWIG. How can the gods make someone so golden, so beautiful, so Lohengrin — so not?

SOPHIE. My poor Ludwig.

LUDWIG. And in the last six months, I have also been to bed with two Tristans, three Tannhausers, five Parsifals and seven-and-a-half Siegfrieds.

SOPHIE. Seven-and-a-half?

LUDWIG. Understudy.

SOPHIE. Of course.

LUDWIG. Is this what you want to marry? *(Pfeiffer enters, carrying a large, velvet-covered box.)*

PFEIFFER. Your Highness?

LUDWIG. Yes?

PFEIFFER. This has just arrived, from St. Petersburg. *(Pfeiffer hands Ludwig the box, and exits.)*

SOPHIE. What's that?

LUDWIG. *(Opening the box.)* My reliquary.

SOPHIE. A reliquary? Why?

LUDWIG. Because the human heart, the actual organ, it's so hidden and ugly. I was hoping that mine, at least after I died, might become beautiful. And it could be placed in a shrine, where people could pray to it, and lose weight. *(Ludwig takes out the reliquary, which is indeed very beautiful. It's a heart-shaped container in hammered gold, encrusted with precious gems.)*

SOPHIE. But it's all wrong.

LUDWIG. Why?

SOPHIE. Because your heart is so much larger.

LUDWIG. It is?

SOPHIE. Ludwig, I do love you, I will always love you. But I can't marry you.

LUDWIG. You can't?

SOPHIE. You've postponed our wedding for years, and you're not even attracted to women. But none of that matters, because you've given me the most wonderful gift.

LUDWIG. What?

SOPHIE. You're the only person who's ever made me feel beautiful.

LUDWIG. I have?

SOPHIE. Thanks to you, I'm the most beautiful humpback in Europe. I hold my head high. Er. I am envied. Imitated. And men have noticed.

LUDWIG. Which men?

SOPHIE. Among others, a certain French nobleman.

LUDWIG. Not Count D'Amboise, that absolute dreamboat?

SOPHIE. *Mais oui.*

LUDWIG. I hate you!

SOPHIE. I wish I could shrug.

LUDWIG. Sophie? *(He gives her the reliquary.)* Take this away. I don't need it. I don't deserve it.

SOPHIE. But why not?

LUDWIG. *(After a beat.)* I'm a terrible king.

SOPHIE. *(After a beat.)* You're absolutely right.

LUDWIG. I daydreamed my way through the war.

SOPHIE. You vanish for months at a time.

LUDWIG. The newspapers call me "Ludwig the Strange," "Ludwig the Spendthrift" ...

SOPHIE. "Ludwig the Slut."

LUDWIG. "Ludwig the Slut"?

SOPHIE. *The Daily Bavarian.*

LUDWIG. No!

SOPHIE. And Parliament has formed a committee to investigate your sanity.

LUDWIG. My sanity?

SOPHIE. Imagine.

LUDWIG. Everything I was born to become, every expectation, every test, every opportunity to justify my existence — I haven't even come close. And I have no excuse.

SOPHIE. Ludwig?

LUDWIG. And I have no choice. I'm going to abdicate.

SOPHIE. What?

LUDWIG. I'm going to leave the throne.

SOPHIE. But that isn't the answer. That's insane.

LUDWIG. Like my grandfather? I'll have Pfeiffer draw up the papers. *(Calling out.)* Pfeiffer!

SOPHIE. So you'll never get there.

LUDWIG. Where?

SOPHIE. Valhalla.

LUDWIG. *(Desperately, at the end of his rope.)* Valhalla doesn't exist! *(Calling out, into the darkness of the theater.)* Pfeiffer! Where is he?

SOPHIE. Ludwig, what do kings do?

LUDWIG. They abdicate. *Pfeiffer!*

SOPHIE. I'm talking about true kings, legendary kings, our kings. Ramses. Alexander. Louis XIV.

LUDWIG. *(She's struck a nerve.)* Louis?

SOPHIE. What did they do?

LUDWIG. They soared. They inspired. They dreamed.

SOPHIE. They built.

LUDWIG. What are you babbling about?

SOPHIE. Temples to Apollo. Pyramids to the stars. Gifts to the world.

LUDWIG. The Forbidden City. The Taj Mahal. The Colosseum.

SOPHIE. Versailles.

LUDWIG. *(Moaning, in ecstasy.)* Oooh ...

SOPHIE. Ludwig?

LUDWIG. I'm sorry, but you know that whenever I hear the word "Versailles," I just get so aroused ...

SOPHIE. That's your genius.

LUDWIG. It's my curse!

SOPHIE. "Versailles."

LUDWIG. Ooooh ...

SOPHIE. "Versailles."

LUDWIG. Stop it!

SOPHIE. What do you want, what do you most believe in, with every ounce of your immortal soul?

LUDWIG. I believe — that the world should be beautiful. That God wants the world to be beautiful. But it isn't!

SOPHIE. Then make it so. In many ways, you *are* God.

LUDWIG. How?

SOPHIE. Because you're no good at reality, but you're brilliant at everything else.

LUDWIG. I am?

SOPHIE. Do for the world what you've done for me. And if people, if parents, if politicians, if they call that madness, well then, my darling ...

LUDWIG. What?

SOPHIE. Go mad. *(Sophie tosses the reliquary back to Ludwig, who catches it.)*

SOPHIE. *Au revoir. (Sophie exits.)*

LUDWIG. What is she talking about? I'm supposed to transform the world? People would think I was crazy. They already do. All right, what are the signs of madness? Number one — do I talk to myself? No. Does madness run in my family? Of course not! Well, except for my grandfather, fifty-eight cousins, three great-aunts, and my brother. Poor Otto — who for the past fifteen years has been chained in his room, where he barks like a dog.

OTTO. *(From offstage, barking.)* Ruff, ruff!

LUDWIG. *(To Otto.)* Sit! The third sign — do I hear voices? Sounds that aren't there? No! I'm not crazy, and I'm leaving the theater, and the throne! Goodbye! *(Ludwig shuts off all the theater's lights, strides off the stage and begins to exit, down the aisle and out through the house. Just as he is almost gone, we hear a single note of music. Ludwig pauses.)* I didn't hear that. No, I'm fine. *(Another few notes are heard.)* It's just the wind in the rafters. It's an old building. Please. *(More Wagnerian music is heard, intoxicating and irresistible. Ludwig clamps his hands over his ears and babbles, trying to shut out the music.)* Lalalalala ... shut up! Shut up! *(Ludwig marches back onstage and speaks to the theater.)* The theater is empty! There's no performance this evening, it's a dark night! I'm not listening! And I'm not building anything! I don't love you! I'm not mad! *(As the music soars, a strong, brilliantly vivid shaft of light appears center stage. Ludwig circles the light, drawn to it, but unsure. With the music urging him onwards, he tentatively puts his hand into the shaft of light. Finally, as the music peaks, Ludwig steps into the light, so it fully illuminates him. He raises his face to the light, his eyes shut, completely surrendering to the glorious allure of the music. Silence. Ludwig opens his eyes. He smiles.)* I'm the king. *(James enters, from the wings.)*

JAMES. Henry Lee? *(Henry Lee enters. He looks out, seeing what James is seeing.)*

HENRY LEE. What is that?

LUDWIG. Pfeiffer? *(Pfeiffer enters.)*

PFEIFFER. Your Highness? *(The two couples will not see each other, but will see the same things.)*

LUDWIG. I want to build something, in the Graswang Valley. Something — rococo.

JAMES. It looks like a huge, demented wedding cake ...

HENRY LEE. With white marble frosting ...

PFEIFFER. But you have a perfectly nice estate here in Munich, why do you need another?

LUDWIG. Just wait.

JAMES. Come on.

HENRY LEE. James?

LUDWIG. And underneath the palace, completely hidden, I want — a shocking surprise. I want to excavate, to hollow out at least a full acre ...

JAMES. There's a secret door, in the side of that hill ...

HENRY LEE. We shouldn't go in there ...

PFEIFFER. But what will be in there?

LUDWIG. Think Hansel and Gretel. Think the *Arabian Nights*.

HENRY LEE. There's a tunnel ...

JAMES. And a trap door ...

LUDWIG. Think *Tannhauser*. Think orgies. *(The four men look around them, having entered an underground grotto. The grotto, and all of the subsequent castles, will involve absolutely no scenery. The locations and their beauty will be established entirely through the characters' words, their delighted reactions and lighting effects.)*

JAMES, HENRY LEE and PFEIFFER. It's a grotto!

LUDWIG. Indeed. First we'll fill the entire cavern with an iron armature, and then cover it with plaster and cement ...

JAMES. It's like a stage set, it's all molded and painted to look like it's carved out of coral ...

PFEIFFER. This sounds costly ...

HENRY LEE. This cost a bundle ...

LUDWIG. Get me the checkbook ...

JAMES. I feel so rich!

HENRY LEE. And look, there are fake stalagtites dripping from the ceiling ...

LUDWIG. Draped with endless garlands of lush plaster blooms ...

PFEIFFER. Perhaps roses and lilies ...

JAMES. There's honeysuckle and hibiscus ...

LUDWIG. I want an artificial Eden ...

HENRY LEE. Don't you think it's kind of spooky?

PFEIFFER. Will your mother be allowed down here?

LUDWIG and JAMES. No!

JAMES. And oh my God, over there, across the whole damn grotto, they built ...

LUDWIG and HENRY LEE. A lake!

PFEIFFER. You want a full-scale, manmade, underground lake?

LUDWIG. With fifty swans and a story-high waterfall ...

JAMES. And there's a machine to make waves ...

HENRY LEE. We could surf!

LUDWIG. I want nature only better ...

PFEIFFER. It's like nature only more expensive ...

HENRY LEE. It's like nature ...

JAMES. If God was gay.

EVERYONE. Yes! *(As the group describes the following lighting effects, they occur, drenching the stage in the most vivid colors.)*

LUDWIG. And I want thousands of hidden lightbulbs to create a continual rainbow, from burning amber ...

HENRY LEE. To popsicle purple …

PFEIFFER. To cockatoo green …

JAMES. And Cadillac blue …

HENRY LEE. *(To James.)* Stop it.

LUDWIG. I will create architecture …

PFEIFFER. As aphrodisiac …

JAMES. Just being down here makes me feel sort of secret clubhouse sexy …

HENRY LEE. And pirate hideout horny …

JAMES. Henry Lee?

PFEIFFER. It's outrageous!

HENRY LEE. Did I say that?

LUDWIG. It's erotic …

JAMES. Yes you did!

LUDWIG. Let's see Parisian-whorehouse, pagan-fire-dance, sex-with-the-devil, lusty-lick-me-red! *(The stage bursts into a fiery scarlet as the music soars.)*

EVERYONE. *WHOA!*

HENRY LEE. James?

JAMES. Henry Lee?

PFEIFFER. Your Highness?

LUDWIG. Pfeiffer?

EVERYONE. I think I have a boner …

LUDWIG. So it's working …

JAMES. This is great!

LUDWIG. But I'm only getting started …

PFEIFFER. Your Highness, please don't say that …

HENRY LEE. I think I kind of like this …

LUDWIG. I think that I'm in love …

JAMES. *(To Henry Lee.)* You do?

HENRY LEE. It's true …

PFEIFFER. *(To Ludwig.)* With who?

JAMES. *(To Henry Lee.)* You too?

LUDWIG. With me! *(As Ludwig strides offstage, followed by Pfeiffer, James and Henry Lee grab each other for a passionate kiss. Natalie Kippelbaum enters. She is a modern-day tour guide, a peppy American woman from Long Island. She wears a gold lamé jogging suit, accessorized with a large button which says "GUIDE," a leopard-skin fanny pack, a majorly highlighted hairdo, plenty of jewelry, over-sized eyeglasses and hot-pink-and-silver-lamé sneakers. Natalie is a born entertainer and hostess, thrilled to share her enthusiasm for*

Ludwig and his castles. She is played by the same actress who plays the Queen. James and Henry Lee exit, as Natalie speaks to the audience and her unseen tour group.)

NATALIE. Hi! I'm Natalie Kippelbaum, and welcome to Temple Beth Shalom's Whirlwind European Adventure Castles of Bavaria Plus Wine Tasting and Wienerschnitzel Potpourri Tour. Yes. The bus will be here any second, so let's get started. And I know what you're thinking, you're going, Natalie, from Long Island, what are you doing with Ludwig? Well, three years ago, I hit bottom. First, my husband, he dies, from lung cancer. Fun. And then, my daughter, she loses her job. Then my son, Debbie — enough said. And I'm in my Hyundai, and I'm about to drive off a bridge, like in a Hyundai that's even necessary, and then — I hear music. Gorgeous, operatic music. You know — NPR. And I think, where is that music coming from, I mean, where was it born? So I get on a plane, and I'm here. And the minute I step into that grotto — I'm happy. I'm high. And today we're going to see something even more beautiful, because in 1883, Ludwig decided to build his copy of Versailles. *(She pronounces the word with a thick Long Island accent — "Versoy.")* That's right — Versailles. *(Ludwig enters, now dressed in a glittering waistcoat, pantaloons and a high, curled wig, as Louis XIV, followed by Pfeiffer, who is also dressed in period French style.)*

PFEIFFER. A copy of Versailles?

NATALIE. We're here! Everybody out! Mrs. Kloper, use your walker!

LUDWIG. It's my ecstatic tribute to Louis XIV, le Roi du Soleil.

NATALIE. And why was Louis called the Sun King? Anyone?

PFEIFFER. He was the center of the solar system.

NATALIE. Good answer, Mrs. Weinblatt.

LUDWIG. You're starting to catch on.

NATALIE. And we're moving ...

LUDWIG. *(As he looks at the palace.)* It's so moving.

PFEIFFER. I'm getting nervous ...

NATALIE. And we're not touching anything ...

LUDWIG. It touches me ...

PFEIFFER. And I'm trembling ...

NATALIE. Here it comes ...

PFEIFFER. And what's in here?

LUDWIG. You may wish to shield your eyes ...

NATALIE. Does anyone have a heart condition?

LUDWIG. May I present, in all its radiant splendor, the heartbeat of the monarchy — the royal bedchamber.

PFEIFFER. *(Seeing it.)* You have outdone yourself.

NATALIE. Look at that bed, I'm palpitating, I'm flushed …

LUDWIG. It's entirely gilded in 24-Karat gold …

NATALIE. It took Parisian artisans over two years to carve …

LUDWIG. It's fit for Louis and his queen …

PFEIFFER. It's fit for Siegfried and Brunhilde …

LUDWIG. It's fit for Venus and Apollo …

NATALIE. Donald Trump, eat shit and die! *(The bed has appeared. James and Henry Lee are in the bed; they now wear their t-shirts and army uniform trousers.)*

HENRY LEE. I can't believe this. We just had sex.

NATALIE. *(Gesturing to the bed.)* Can you imagine? For sex?

JAMES. Did you like it?

LUDWIG. Pure silk sheets …

HENRY LEE. While we were doing it, I sort of forgot who I was …

NATALIE. Forget about it …

HENRY LEE. And where I was …

PFEIFFER. That bed is evil …

JAMES. Is that bad?

LUDWIG. Is it heaven?

HENRY LEE. It's just new … .

NATALIE. It just kills me …

HENRY LEE. It's just crazy …

JAMES. So what do you think?

HENRY LEE. It's amazing.

JAMES, LUDWIG and PFEIFFER. It's spectacular!

NATALIE. It's Bed, Bath and Beyond!

PFEIFFER. Your Highness — enough.

LUDWIG. Enough?

NATALIE. So people, let me ask you — do you think we've had enough?

PFEIFFER. They're going to say that you've gone mad …

HENRY LEE. They're gonna say that we went AWOL …

NATALIE. Someone's gotta say it — are we fatootsed?

JAMES and LUDWIG. Maybe you're right …

NATALIE. Mrs. Kloper, am I right?

HENRY LEE. I mean, what about our mission?

PFEIFFER. And Bismarck's coalition?

NATALIE. Are we having a conniption?

JAMES. Should we check our ammunition?

LUDWIG. I shall tell you my position.

HENRY LEE. But there's just one thing I'm wishin' ...

JAMES. What?

LUDWIG. More.

PFEIFFER. More?

HENRY LEE. More.

JAMES. More?

NATALIE. More? So what do we think?

EVERYONE. *More! (The ghost of Marie Antoinette appears, wearing a high, powdered wig, jewels and a sumptuous gown. Only Ludwig will be able to see her. Marie will be played by the same actress who plays Sally.)*

MARIE. *Bonjour.*

LUDWIG. *(Delighted.)* Your Majesty!

MARIE. Your Highness.

PFEIFFER. *(To Ludwig.)* Who are you talking to?

LUDWIG. For throwing a truly memorable ball, for all the crowned heads of Europe, the queen requires, the planet requires, my soul requires — a Hall of Mirrors. *(The stage is filled with a zillion shards of reflected light, as from a series of mirror balls, so the light dances. James and Henry Lee climb out of bed, and join the group in responding to the light.)*

JAMES and HENRY LEE. Oh my God ...

PFEIFFER and NATALIE. Oh my God ...

MARIE. People always say that ...

LUDWIG. There are over 12,000 separate panes of mirror ...

NATALIE. Count the fifteen crystal chandeliers ...

HENRY LEE. It's like getting lost inside a diamond ...

PFEIFFER. Everywhere I turn, I see myself ...

MARIE. *(To the group.)* Look, it's you ...

EVERYONE. *(Seeing themselves in the mirrors.)* Look, it's me ...

JAMES. *(To Henry Lee.)* Look, it's us ...

NATALIE. Can't you just see Marie Antoinette?

JAMES. It's like in that movie, *Marie Antoinette* ...

PFEIFFER. Your Highness, what are you looking at?

LUDWIG. Just the beautiful Marie Antoinette ...

MARIE. *Merci.*

NATALIE. Although in her portraits, her hips are so huge ...

MARIE. It's the dress! *(Marie pinches Natalie.)*

NATALIE. *(Reacting to the pinch; she doesn't see Marie.)* Mrs. Kloper?

HENRY LEE. I think I read that she was vain ...

MARIE. Not vain, French! *(Marie slaps Henry Lee on the back of his head.)*

HENRY LEE. *(Reacting to the slap.)* James?

JAMES. What?

PFEIFFER. They put her head on a spike!

MARIE. Don't remind me! *(Marie kicks Pfeiffer.)*

PFEIFFER. *(Reacting to the kick.)* Your Highness?

LUDWIG. *(To Marie.)* But you still look great!

MARIE. We would always have such dancing …

NATALIE and JAMES. This place is made for dancing …

LUDWIG. I will create an orchestra, for dancing …

HENRY LEE and NATALIE. What did they call it?

JAMES, LUDWIG and PFEIFFER. The gavotte! *(A sparkling gavotte or minuet is heard.)*

LUDWIG and MARIE. *Mais oui!*

NATALIE. This music is available in the gift shop, on CD, along with postcards, slide sets and commemorative plates and keychains …

LUDWIG. *(Bowing to Marie.)* Your Highness?

JAMES. *(Bowing to Henry Lee.)* Private Stafford?

PFEIFFER. I'm so alone …

NATALIE. The snack bar is to your left …

JAMES and LUDWIG. Shall we dance?

MARIE and HENRY LEE. I couldn't.

JAMES and LUDWIG. But why not?

NATALIE. And the restrooms are on your right …

HENRY LEE. I'm a soldier …

MARIE and PFEIFFER. It's been so long …

HENRY LEE. We're at war …

MARIE. I have no head …

NATALIE. I'm thinking about my husband …

PFEIFFER. I'm thinking about my Valkyrie …

MARIE. I'm thinking about my Louis …

JAMES. That's the reason …

LUDWIG. This is your ballroom …

NATALIE. He was a fabulous dancer. He'd say to me, "Natalie … "

PFEIFFER. *(Turning to Natalie.)* Brunhilde?

NATALIE. *(To Pfeiffer.)* Myron?

JAMES. Henry Lee?

LUDWIG. Marie?

EVERYONE. Let's dance! *(The group begins to dance a gavotte, in couples: James and Henry Lee, Ludwig and Marie, Pfeiffer and Natalie.*

Then the music grows livelier, turning into a World War II swing anthem, something like "Sing, Sing, Sing." Everyone breaks into an exuberant jitterbug. As Natalie steps forward, everyone else dances offstage.)
NATALIE. Ludwig couldn't stop building — he was hooked, like on crack. He would race from one construction site to the next, at midnight in a sleigh drawn by six white stallions — goyim! He did a Moorish pavilion, a medieval hunting lodge, and a theater at Bayreuth, with perfect acoustics, where the works of Richard Wagner are still performed to this day. And I know, that Wagner, he was no friend of the Jews. So you know what I call him? *(She uses the soft, American "W")* Wagner. Dickie Wagner. Ha! He'd die! He did! What's that, Mrs. Slatkin? So what happened to Ludwig? You'll see in just a minute, when we make our final stop. But just remember, if you can't give up everything, even your life itself, for what you truly believe in, well, then why bother? So whenever I'm down, whenever I think about terrorists and starving children and Debbie trying to find shoes — I think of Ludwig. So grab your bottled water and your Instamatics, and look out your window, on the left, because here it comes, all the way up on that mountaintop, it's Ludwig's ultimate dream, his home of the gods, his swansong, I'm kvelling, wait till you see it, if it were a person, I'd have sex with it, and I'm not a young woman. There it is — excuse me, I need a moment. *(She takes a deep breath, composing herself, overcome.)* There it is — Valhalla! *(As Natalie exits, Ludwig enters, dressed as a highly theatrical medieval knight, in armor and velvet. He looks out, and up.)*
LUDWIG. I like to ride out here, at least a mile away, and just gaze up at it. It was finished today. *(Pfeiffer enters, dressed in an outlandish velvet costume, with a tunic, pantaloons and a plumed hat.)*
PFEIFFER. But why are we dressed like this?
LUDWIG. At last, I am Lohengrin. *(James runs on, and stares up at the mountaintop.)*
JAMES. What is that? *(Henry Lee enters.)*
HENRY LEE. I can't see it.
JAMES. The clouds are in the way.
LUDWIG. *(Pointing.)* And next, even higher up the mountain, I'm going to build a temple to Apollo, a parthenon, made entirely of glass. And then I think a pagoda, and something Hindu, and — a Sphinx.
PFEIFFER. Your Highness?
HENRY LEE. I got a letter. I've been carrying it around ever since

we got overseas. I've been afraid to open it.

LUDWIG. Yes?

JAMES. Why?

HENRY LEE. It's from Sally.

PFEIFFER. You've been building without pause for over ten years. You've spent every Deustche mark you own, and the royal treasury is over five million in debt.

LUDWIG. What are you saying? *(Lights up on Sally, in a simple dress.)*

JAMES. *(Reading the letter aloud.)* "Dear Henry Lee and James … "

SALLY. Somehow I know that you've found each other. And I don't know if I'm jealous, or relieved. But I do know this — James, I wish I didn't love you. And Henry Lee, I wish I could love you more. And please, take care of each other, and stay safe. And don't worry about me, because I'm going to have plenty of company. I'm going to have a baby.

PFEIFFER. You have no more money. *(The Queen enters.)*

QUEEN. Ludwig?

LUDWIG. Mother?

QUEEN. There are soldiers at the gatehouse. With a warrant for your arrest.

LUDWIG. Why?

QUEEN. Parliament has had you declared — insane.

LUDWIG. I don't believe you.

QUEEN. And unfit to rule.

SALLY. One of you is going to be a father.

JAMES. "Love, Sally." *(Sally exits.)*

HENRY LEE. A baby.

JAMES. Go back. Radio the base.

HENRY LEE. I should. I know that.

JAMES. You have a war. And a wife. And a family. And a future.

HENRY LEE. You make all of that sound so impossible. As if no one should ever want those things.

JAMES. I'm not asking you to choose. Not anymore.

HENRY LEE. But what will happen to you?

JAMES. Everything else.

HENRY LEE. You'll be alone.

JAMES. Maybe. But since we got here, to Bavaria, have you noticed something?

HENRY LEE. What?

JAMES. I haven't taken anything. We've been in all of these castles, filled with treasures, and — nothing.

HENRY LEE. But why not?

JAMES. Because from now on, everywhere I go, everything I see, the whole world — it's all mine.

LUDWIG. But there must be money somewhere, to be borrowed or raised. How can anyone see my castles, and not wish for more?

QUEEN. You must prepare yourself.

PFEIFFER. You must defend yourself.

LUDWIG. Why?

QUEEN. The committee claims to have evidence of your dementia. They say that you spend hours speaking to the ghost of Marie Antoinette.

LUDWIG. I adore her.

QUEEN. They say that you hire gilded stableboys to row you about your grotto, in a boat shaped like a duck.

LUDWIG. A swan.

QUEEN. And that you were glimpsed on a hillside, reciting the Song of Solomon, while dressed as a nun.

LUDWIG. It was Sunday!

QUEEN. Ludwig. My sweet boy,

LUDWIG. But who has reported all of this? Who has betrayed me?

QUEEN. A friend.

PFEIFFER. I'm sorry.

LUDWIG. Pfeiffer? *(The Queen exits.)*

HENRY LEE. James?

JAMES. Yeah?

HENRY LEE. I have never hated anyone the way I've hated you.

JAMES. I'm blushing.

HENRY LEE. Since that very first night, when we were kids — you have pushed me.

JAMES. Out of Dainsville.

HENRY LEE. And you have mocked me.

JAMES. Someone had to.

HENRY LEE. And you have tried to make me — like you.

JAMES. You are like me!

HENRY LEE. No I'm not! I don't have half your imagination. Or your courage.

JAMES. Henry Lee?

HENRY LEE. And I'm nowhere near as annoying.

JAMES. Because you don't apply yourself.

LUDWIG. But I'm the king. I have dreamed. I have unleashed my fullest imagination, to create — the purest beauty on this earth.

Anyone, everyone can see that. Just look!

JAMES. Look. *(Everyone onstage now faces out, gazing up at Valhalla Castle, as the clouds clear. The view is breathtaking.)*

PFEIFFER. The turrets ...

HENRY LEE. And the towers ...

JAMES. The banners ...

LUDWIG. And the gold ...

PFEIFFER. It's El Dorado ...

LUDWIG. It's Nirvana ...

HENRY LEE. It's Olympus ...

JAMES. No, it's Oz ...

PFEIFFER. I love this mountain ...

JAMES. I love this morning ...

HENRY LEE. I love this world.

LUDWIG. I love my dreams ...

PFEIFFER. I can't stop looking ...

LUDWIG. My soul is bursting ...

JAMES. That is the opposite of Texas!

PFEIFFER. It soars!

JAMES. It floats!

LUDWIG. It sings!

HENRY LEE. James?

JAMES. Yeah?

HENRY LEE. I'm coming with you. All the way.

JAMES. Why?

HENRY LEE. Because I'm going to say the most dangerous thing I can think of.

JAMES. What?

HENRY LEE. That the world is beautiful.

LUDWIG. Am I mad?

JAMES. So do you love me?

HENRY LEE. What?

JAMES. Do you love me?

HENRY LEE. Why?

JAMES. Do you love me?

HENRY LEE. If I say yes, will it make you just way too happy?

JAMES. Find out.

LUDWIG. *(Gesturing to Valhalla.)* If all this, if all of my dreams, if my entire life is pure insanity; then I have only one response —

HENRY LEE. Yes.

JAMES. Yes!

LUDWIG. *Yes. (We hear a musical phrase from* Lohengrin. *Everyone onstage hears it.)*

HENRY LEE. Listen.

PFEIFFER. Listen.

JAMES. What is that?

LUDWIG. It's the "Prelude," from *Lohengrin.*

HENRY LEE. It sounds like — the beginning of something. *(Henry Lee goes to James. As they are about to embrace, a shot rings out. The bullet hits Henry Lee, who crumples, and then stands and walks offstage. We hear a Wagnerian crescendo. Blackout. Lights up on Margaret, in Texas. She brings a straightback chair onstage and stands behind it. She speaks to an unseen reporter.)*

MARGARET. Yes, I'm James Avery's mother. Excuse me? No, I'm sorry, but this is not a concern of your newspaper. Or of anyone else outside our immediate family. You are misinformed — James did not go AWOL. He was honorably discharged, following a complete and severe emotional breakdown. He had seen Henry Lee Stafford killed before his very eyes. He served his country, he is lucky to be alive, and that is all there is to it. Have I made myself clear? Thank you. Good afternoon. *(Margaret exits. Ludwig enters and sits in the straightback chair. He wears somewhat disheveled, ordinary black clothing, as does Pfeiffer, who stands nearby.)*

PFEIFFER. Do you understand what has happened?

LUDWIG. Thanks to you and your confederates?

PFEIFFER. I'm sorry, I can go, but I've asked the committee if I could stay with you.

LUDWIG. And you shall. You shall witness. That I am imprisoned here, at Valhalla. With holes drilled in every door.

PFEIFFER. Only for observation.

LUDWIG. While my brother Otto has been placed on the throne.

PFEIFFER. Only as a symbol.

LUDWIG. Does he get his own dish? *(Ludwig and Pfeiffer remain onstage. James enters, and sits elsewhere; he's now behind the counter at his family's hardware store in Dainsville. He wears civilian clothes and speaks to an unseen reporter.)*

JAMES. … oh thank you, I'm feeling much better, six months in the VA hospital, good as new. Yes, it was terrible about Henry Lee, I feel so — responsible, somehow. No, no, it's okay, put it in the paper, I want people to know. You see, he was shot by a Nazi soldier, a boy who just a few days before, I had let — live. And after he shot Henry Lee, he just stood there, a few yards away, staring at me. Daring me.

PFEIFFER. Your Highness, Ludwig, I'm sorry, I'm not sure of the proper form of address ...

LUDWIG. Your Madness.

PFEIFFER. I know this is difficult, but it's only been a day.

LUDWIG. They will never let me out. And they will never let me build.

PFEIFFER. I know.

JAMES. And I shot him. And I kept shooting, until our platoon sergeant found me, three days later, outside this big castle. He said that it was like I was guarding it. And I guess I'd ... I'd had enough, and I collapsed. And at the hospital I decided that maybe, if I came right back here to Dainsville, I could — well, nobody can take Henry Lee's place, but I can do — what he might've done. So I'm taking over my dad's hardware store, and from now on, I'm a Texas boy. Sally came in, just the other day, with the baby. A little girl. And I held her. She looks just like — her mom. Speaking of which, would you like to see something? Something beautiful?

LUDWIG. Do you think I'm crazy?

PFEIFFER. I think that you're — like opera.

LUDWIG. Why?

PFEIFFER. Because opera is music that's gone mad.

LUDWIG. Could you get permission, for a walk by the lake? Tell them that you will accompany me — as a chaperone. *(Ludwig and Pfeiffer exit; Pfeiffer takes the chair offstage with him. James now holds an object wrapped in burlap.)*

JAMES. Now I can't tell you exactly how I came by this, but ... *(He takes out Ludwig's reliquary.)* Yes, it's pure gold. It's called a reliquary, yes, I know it's shaped like a heart, but inside — it's the real thing. Well, I guess it is kind of, what did you say, gruesome, but it's almost one hundred years old, and that's how they did it back then, at least for royalty, you know, bigshots. They would bury the body, but the heart, that was precious. *(Ludwig walks onstage, now wearing a homburg and a long black overcoat.)*

LUDWIG. Pfeiffer, come along! *(He gazes out at the lake, towards the audience.)* Look at that. The water. Like glass. How deep is this?

JAMES. *(As the unseen reporter leaves.)* Goodbye.

LUDWIG. *(Still to Pfeiffer, who remains offstage.)* Lohengrin — remember? At the end, after the knight has been betrayed, his ship appears, and he sails off alone. *(The two men can now see and hear each other.)*

JAMES. Hey.

LUDWIG. Yes?

JAMES. Your Highness.

LUDWIG. James.

JAMES. They found your body the next day.

LUDWIG. When they dragged the lake.

JAMES. Why?

LUDWIG. Because the world is an ugly place, filled with ugly people. And it has nothing to do with physical appearance.

JAMES. There are pretty Nazis.

LUDWIG. And the loveliest humpbacks.

JAMES. So what should we do? Build our own worlds?

LUDWIG. No! My life was utterly selfish. A complete fraud. A waste.

JAMES. Why?

LUDWIG. I was alone. And you stole my heart.

JAMES. I needed it.

LUDWIG. Why?

JAMES. Because you left something out of the story. As Lohengrin sails off, he performs — a final miracle.

LUDWIG. I love miracles.

JAMES. The swan vanishes, and in its place, on the riverbank, there appears ...

LUDWIG. The maiden's brother. At last! *(Annie Avery, a young woman dressed in the style of the early 1970s, enters. She will be played by the same actress who plays Sally. She moves center stage and speaks to an unseen official. As she speaks, James will hand her the reliquary.)*

ANNIE. Hi, I'm Annie Avery. And I know this is really weird, but, well, last year, my dad passed away, from cancer. But before he died, he made me swear that I would return this. He said that it was the only way that he could be absolutely sure that I would see — the most beautiful place on earth. I'm sorry, are you the right person? Are you in charge, here at the castle?

LUDWIG. *(Turning to her.)* Yes.

ANNIE. *(Looking around, in awe.)* Well, Jesus. I wish my mom could see this, but she hasn't been well. She loved my dad so much, and I promised I'd tell her all about this.

LUDWIG. Then you must. And I believe there are postcards.

JAMES. *(Just to Ludwig.)* And mugs. They say, "I Love Ludwig."

LUDWIG. *(To Annie.)* And mugs.

ANNIE. *(Still looking around.)* Well, my God, for my mom, and my dad, and for everybody — thank you.

LUDWIG. Of course. And, back in ...

ANNIE. Texas.

LUDWIG. What do you do?

ANNIE. I work in the public schools. I teach.

LUDWIG. Yes?

ANNIE. Music.

LUDWIG. *(Referring to the reliquary.)* Open it.

ANNIE. I'm afraid that I already have. It's empty.

LUDWIG. Try again. *(Annie opens the reliquary. Inside, nestled in velvet, she finds the crystal swan, which James had stolen in the play's opening moments. She holds the swan up to the light, where it glistens.)*

ANNIE. It's beautiful. *(As music from* Lohengrin *fills the theater, James and Ludwig watch Annie; they are very pleased. Curtain.)*

End of Play

PROPERTY LIST

Crystal swan (JAMES)
Wrapped bundle with book and flashlight (JAMES)
Pocket watch (QUEEN)
Rubber ball (OTTO)
Plate of cookies (SALLY)
Football (HENRY LEE)
Fan (URSULA)
Brush, makeup (SALLY)
Pistols (LUDWIG, SOPHIE)
Golden scepter, piece of paper (LUDWIG)
Sawed-off shotgun (REVEREND)
Bouquet (JAMES)
Sheaf of documents (PFIEFFER)
Handcuffs (LUDWIG)
Cigarettes (JAMES and HENRY LEE)
White horse and sword (LUDWIG)
Black horse and sword (QUEEN)
Parachutes (HENRY LEE and JAMES)
Binoculars (JAMES)
Walkie-talkie (HENRY LEE)
Pistol (JAMES)
Large velvet-covered box with gold reliquary (PFEIFFER)
Letter (JAMES)
Straightback chair (MARGARET)
Reliquary with crystal swan wrapped in burlap (JAMES)

SOUND EFFECTS

Wagnerian music
Police siren
Metal doors clanging shut
Rushing water
Gunshots
Romantic music
Processional music, roaring crowd
"Wedding March"
Selection from *Tannhauser*
Ship's bell, ocean sounds
Enchanted music
Villainous music
Siren, dogs barkings
Machine-gun fire and music
Gavotte
Swing music
"Prelude" from *Lohengrin*

NEW PLAYS

★ **MONTHS ON END by Craig Pospisil.** In comic scenes, one for each month of the year, we follow the intertwined worlds of a circle of friends and family whose lives are poised between happiness and heartbreak. "...a triumph...these twelve vignettes all form crucial pieces in the eternal puzzle known as human relationships, an area in which the playwright displays an assured knowledge that spans deep sorrow to unbounded happiness." *—Ann Arbor News.* "...rings with emotional truth, humor...[an] endearing contemplation on love...entertaining and satisfying." *—Oakland Press.* [5M, 5W] ISBN: 0-8222-1892-5

★ **GOOD THING by Jessica Goldberg.** Brings us into the households of John and Nancy Roy, forty-something high-school guidance counselors whose marriage has been increasingly on the rocks and Dean and Mary, recent graduates struggling to make their way in life. "...a blend of gritty social drama, poetic humor and unsubtle existential contemplation..." *—Variety.* [3M, 3W] ISBN: 0-8222-1869-0

★ **THE DEAD EYE BOY by Angus MacLachlan.** Having fallen in love at their Narcotics Anonymous meeting, Billy and Shirley-Diane are striving to overcome the past together. But their relationship is complicated by the presence of Sorin, Shirley-Diane's fourteen-year-old son, a damaged reminder of her dark past. "...a grim, insightful portrait of an unmoored family..." *—NY Times.* "MacLachlan's play isn't for the squeamish, but then, tragic stories delivered at such an unrelenting fever pitch rarely are." *—Variety.* [1M, 1W, 1 boy] ISBN: 0-8222-1844-5

★ **[SIC] by Melissa James Gibson.** In adjacent apartments three young, ambitious neighbors come together to discuss, flirt, argue, share their dreams and plan their futures with unequal degrees of deep hopefulness and abject despair. "A work...concerned with the sound and power of language..." *—NY Times.* "...a wonderfully original take on urban friendship and the comedy of manners—a *Design for Living* for our times..." *—NY Observer.* [3M, 2W] ISBN: 0-8222-1872-0

★ **LOOKING FOR NORMAL by Jane Anderson.** Roy and Irma's twenty-five-year marriage is thrown into turmoil when Roy confesses that he is actually a woman trapped in a man's body, forcing the couple to wrestle with the meaning of their marriage and the delicate dynamics of family. "Jane Anderson's bittersweet transgender domestic comedy-drama ...is thoughtful and touching and full of wit and wisdom. A real audience pleaser." *—Hollywood Reporter.* [5M, 4W] ISBN: 0-8222-1857-7

★ **ENDPAPERS by Thomas McCormack.** The regal Joshua Maynard, the old and ailing head of a mid-sized, family-owned book-publishing house in New York City, must name a successor. One faction in the house backs a smart, "pragmatic" manager, the other faction a smart, "sensitive" editor and both factions fear what the other's man could do to this house— and to them. "If Kaufman and Hart had undertaken a comedy about the publishing business, they might have written *Endpapers*...a breathlessly fast, funny, and thoughtful comedy ...keeps you amused, guessing, and often surprised...profound in its empathy for the paradoxes of human nature." *—NY Magazine.* [7M, 4W] ISBN: 0-8222-1908-5

★ **THE PAVILION by Craig Wright.** By turns poetic and comic, romantic and philosophical, this play asks old lovers to face the consequences of difficult choices made long ago. "The script's greatest strength lies in the genuineness of its feeling." *—Houston Chronicle.* "Wright's perceptive, gently witty writing makes this familiar situation fresh and thoroughly involving." *—Philadelphia Inquirer.* [2M, 1W (flexible casting)] ISBN: 0-8222-1898-4

DRAMATISTS PLAY SERVICE, INC.
440 Park Avenue South, New York, NY 10016 212-683-8960 Fax 212-213-1539
postmaster@dramatists.com www.dramatists.com

NEW PLAYS

★ **BE AGGRESSIVE by Annie Weisman.** Vista Del Sol is paradise, sandy beaches, avocado-lined streets. But for seventeen-year-old cheerleader Laura, everything changes when her mother is killed in a car crash, and she embarks on a journey to the Spirit Institute of the South where she can learn "cheer" with Bible belt intensity. "...filled with lingual gymnastics...stylized rapid-fire dialogue..." *–Variety.* "...a new, exciting, and unique voice in the American theatre..." *–BackStage West.* [1M, 4W, extras] ISBN: 0-8222-1894-1

★ **FOUR by Christopher Shinn.** Four people struggle desperately to connect in this quiet, sophisticated, moving drama. "...smart, broken-hearted...Mr. Shinn has a precocious and forgiving sense of how power shifts in the game of sexual pursuit...He promises to be a playwright to reckon with..." *–NY Times.* "A voice emerges from an American place. It's got humor, sadness and a fresh and touching rhythm that tell of the loneliness and secrets of life...[a] poetic, haunting play." *–NY Post.* [3M, 1W] ISBN: 0-8222-1850-X

★ **WONDER OF THE WORLD by David Lindsay-Abaire.** A madcap picaresque involving Niagara Falls, a lonely tour-boat captain, a pair of bickering private detectives and a husband's dirty little secret. "Exceedingly whimsical and playfully wicked. Winning and genial. A top-drawer production." *–NY Times.* "Full frontal lunacy is on display. A most assuredly fresh and hilarious tragicomedy of marital discord run amok...absolutely hysterical..." *–Variety.* [3M, 4W (doubling)] ISBN: 0-8222-1863-1

★ **QED by Peter Parnell.** Nobel Prize-winning physicist and all-around genius Richard Feynman holds forth with captivating wit and wisdom in this fascinating biographical play that originally starred Alan Alda. "QED is a seductive mix of science, human affections, moral courage, and comic eccentricity. It reflects on, among other things, death, the absence of God, travel to an unexplored country, the pleasures of drumming, and the need to know and understand." *–NY Magazine.* "Its rhythms correspond to the way that people—even geniuses—approach and avoid highly emotional issues, and it portrays Feynman with affection and awe." *–The New Yorker.* [1M, 1W] ISBN: 0-8222-1924-7

★ **UNWRAP YOUR CANDY by Doug Wright.** Alternately chilling and hilarious, this deliciously macabre collection of four bedtime tales for adults is guaranteed to keep you awake for nights on end. "Engaging and intellectually satisfying...a treat to watch." *–NY Times.* "Fiendishly clever. Mordantly funny and chilling. Doug Wright teases, freezes and zaps us." *–Village Voice.* "Four bite-size plays that bite back." *–Variety.* [flexible casting] ISBN: 0-8222-1871-2

★ **FURTHER THAN THE FURTHEST THING by Zinnie Harris.** On a remote island in the middle of the Atlantic secrets are buried. When the outside world comes calling, the islanders find their world blown apart from the inside as well as beyond. "Harris winningly produces an intimate and poetic, as well as political, family saga." *–Independent (London).* "Harris' enthralling adventure of a play marks a departure from stale, well-furrowed theatrical terrain." *–Evening Standard (London).* [3M, 2W] ISBN: 0-8222-1874-7

★ **THE DESIGNATED MOURNER by Wallace Shawn.** The story of three people living in a country where what sort of books people like to read and how they choose to amuse themselves becomes both firmly personal and unexpectedly entangled with questions of survival. "This is a playwright who does not just tell you what it is like to be arrested at night by goons or to fall morally apart and become an aimless yet weirdly contented ghost yourself. He has the originality to make you feel it." *–Times (London).* "A fascinating play with beautiful passages of writing..." *–Variety.* [2M, 1W] ISBN: 0-8222-1848-8

DRAMATISTS PLAY SERVICE, INC.
440 Park Avenue South, New York, NY 10016 212-683-8960 Fax 212-213-1539
postmaster@dramatists.com www.dramatists.com

NEW PLAYS

★ **SHEL'S SHORTS by Shel Silverstein.** Lauded poet, songwriter and author of children's books, the incomparable Shel Silverstein's short plays are deeply infused with the same wicked sense of humor that made him famous. "...[a] childlike honesty and twisted sense of humor." *–Boston Herald.* "...terse dialogue and an absurdity laced with a tang of dread give [*Shel's Shorts*] more than a trace of Samuel Beckett's comic existentialism." *–Boston Phoenix.* [flexible casting] ISBN: 0-8222-1897-6

★ **AN ADULT EVENING OF SHEL SILVERSTEIN by Shel Silverstein.** Welcome to the darkly comic world of Shel Silverstein, a world where nothing is as it seems and where the most innocent conversation can turn menacing in an instant. These ten imaginative plays vary widely in content, but the style is unmistakable. "...[*An Adult Evening*] shows off Silverstein's virtuosic gift for wordplay...[and] sends the audience out...with a clear appreciation of human nature as perverse and laughable." *–NY Times.* [flexible casting] ISBN: 0-8222-1873-9

★ **WHERE'S MY MONEY? by John Patrick Shanley.** A caustic and sardonic vivisection of the institution of marriage, laced with the author's inimitable razor-sharp wit. "...Shanley's gift for acid-laced one-liners and emotionally tumescent exchanges is certainly potent..." *–Variety.* "...lively, smart, occasionally scary and rich in reverse wisdom." *–NY Times.* [3M, 3W] ISBN: 0-8222-1865-8

★ **A FEW STOUT INDIVIDUALS by John Guare.** A wonderfully screwy comedy-drama that figures Ulysses S. Grant in the throes of writing his memoirs, surrounded by a cast of fantastical characters, including the Emperor and Empress of Japan, the opera star Adelina Patti and Mark Twain. "Guare's smarts, passion and creativity skyrocket to awesome heights..." *–Star Ledger.* "...precisely the kind of good new play that you might call an everyday miracle...every minute of it is fresh and newly alive..." *–Village Voice.* [10M, 3W] ISBN: 0-8222-1907-7

★ **BREATH, BOOM by Kia Corthron.** A look at fourteen years in the life of Prix, a Bronx native, from her ruthless girl-gang leadership at sixteen through her coming to maturity at thirty. "...vivid world, believable and eye-opening, a place worthy of a dramatic visit, where no one would want to live but many have to." *–NY Times.* "...rich with humor, terse vernacular strength and gritty detail..." *–Variety.* [1M, 9W] ISBN: 0-8222-1849-6

★ **THE LATE HENRY MOSS by Sam Shepard.** Two antagonistic brothers, Ray and Earl, are brought together after their father, Henry Moss, is found dead in his seedy New Mexico home in this classic Shepard tale. "...His singular gift has been for building mysteries out of the ordinary ingredients of American family life..." *–NY Times.* "...rich moments ...Shepard finds gold." *–LA Times.* [7M, 1W] ISBN: 0-8222-1858-5

★ **THE CARPETBAGGER'S CHILDREN by Horton Foote.** One family's history spanning from the Civil War to WWII is recounted by three sisters in evocative, intertwining monologues. "...bittersweet music—[a] rhapsody of ambivalence...in its modest, garrulous way...theatrically daring." *–The New Yorker.* [3W] ISBN: 0-8222-1843-7

★ **THE NINA VARIATIONS by Steven Dietz.** In this funny, fierce and heartbreaking homage to *The Seagull*, Dietz puts Chekhov's star-crossed lovers in a room and doesn't let them out. "A perfect little jewel of a play..." *–Shepherdstown Chronicle.* "...a delightful revelation of a writer at play; and also an odd, haunting, moving theater piece of lingering beauty." *–Eastside Journal (Seattle).* [1M, 1W (flexible casting)] ISBN: 0-8222-1891-7

DRAMATISTS PLAY SERVICE, INC.
440 Park Avenue South, New York, NY 10016 212-683-8960 Fax 212-213-1539
postmaster@dramatists.com www.dramatists.com